DIVIDED GOVERNMENT

SECOND EDITION

MORRIS FIORINA

Harvard University

Allyn and Bacon
Boston • London • Toronto • Sydney • Tokyo • Singapore

Executive Editor, Political Science: Sean Wakely
Senior Editor: Stephen Hull
Editorial Assistant: Susan Hutchinson
Marketing Manager: Karon Bowers
Editorial Production Administrator: Marjorie Payne
Editorial Production Service: Chestnut Hill Enterprises
Composition/Prepress Buyer: Linda Cox
Cover Administrator: Suzanne Harbison

Copyright © 1996 by Allyn & Bacon
A Simon & Schuster Company
Needham Heights, MA 02194
Copyright © 1992 by Morris Fiorina

Library of Congress Cataloging-in-Publication Data
Fiorina, Morris P.
    Divided government / Morris Fiorina. -- 2nd ed.
      p. cm.
    Includes bibliographical references and index.
    ISBN 0-205-19569-5 (alk. paper)
    1. Party affiliation--United States. 2. Political parties--United
States. 3. United States--Politics and government--1945-1989.
4. United States--Politics and government--1989-1993. I. Title
JK2261.F56 1995
320.973--dc20   95-23579
                                                CIP

Printed in the United States of America
10 9 8 7 6 5 4 3 2 1   00 99 98 97 96 95

Contents

PREFACE TO THE SECOND EDITION

My colleague, Sid Verba, has observed that, whenever social scientists think they have a process accurately described or a question satisfactorily answered, it is a sure signal that things are about to change. For example, in the early 1960s sociologists concluded that the ability of economists to fine tune the economy had brought about the "end of ideology." Within a decade, American politics entered a new, ideologically charged period that continues to the present day. In 1973 the Keynesian revolution in macroeconomics was so complete that even Richard Nixon publicly announced his conversion. Within a few years economists decided that Keynesianism no longer worked, as they looked upon "stagflation"—high unemployment combined with high inflation. And in 1980, those who earlier had announced the death of god were dismayed to find that she was alive and well (and according to some, a Republican).

On a more modest scale the first edition of this book is another illustration of Verba's point. When I began to write the book in the winter of 1991, the evening newscasts were filled with pictures of jubilant Kuwaitis marching around with arms upraised chanting "Bush! Bush! Bush!" In the aftermath of the war, Bush's approval ratings soared to historic highs—eventually reaching 90 percent, and potential heavyweight contenders for the Democratic presidential nomination began announcing that they were completely content in their present offices. With Bush looking untouchable and the Democratic base in the House of Representatives seemingly as unshakeable as ever, divided government looked to be as permanent a part of the national political landscape as anything ever is in this world.

Even in the spring of 1992 when the book appeared, the timeliness of the topic seemed assured. Bill Clinton was fighting for his political life in the wake of Gennifer Flowers' revelations, and additional salacious rumors abounded. And if not Clinton, who? President Paul Tsongas? Not likely. President Jerry Brown? Enough said.

That Clinton survived the spring made the prospects for divided government that much better. By June he was running third in the polls, and pundits mused that Perot was the real alternative to Bush. Then came the happy Democratic convention, the unhappy Republican convention, Perot's descent into paranoia, and the reversal of Bush's and Clinton's political stocks. After what is generally viewed as one of the poorer Republican campaigns in memory, the voters allegedly expressed their frustration with "gridlock" and put an end to twelve consecutive years of divided national government by electing Bill Clinton.

From an authorial standpoint, this development, however awkwardly timed, did not trouble me. After all, the election of a Democrat by a 43 percent plurality hardly signalled an end to the national dissensus that I discussed in the book. Counting Perot voters, presidential-congressional ticket-splitting was at an all-time high in 1992, and, even not counting them, ticket-splitting was at a level comparable with that in elections of the 1980s. Many observers believed that the Republicans could very well capture the Senate in 1994, given the competitiveness of Senate elections and the fact that Democrats would be defending two-thirds of the seats at risk with the inexorable off-year tide running against them. Moreover, as detailed in Chapter 9, the 1992 elections did not diminish the frequency of divided government in the states. Quite on the contrary, the elections left state governments arguably more divided than they had been going in. All in all, the 1992 elections indicated little or nothing in the way of fundamental change.

Popular political commentary saw things differently, at least for awhile. After being a major campaign issue, "gridlock" disappeared from political discussion, and divided government became yesterday's news, a subject merely of historical interest. In the initial flush of victory, many journalists and columnists who should have known better became caught up in the belief that Democratic capture of the presidency had put an end to gridlock. As time passed, however, more than a few observers began to notice that the reemergence of unified national government had not worked any miracles, an observation that became universal during the long, messy death of the Clinton health-care proposals.

And then came the 1994 elections. Just as 1992 had ended the era of divided national government by breaking the Republican lock on the presidency, so 1994 restored divided national government by breaking the Democratic lock on the Congress and the House of Representatives in particular. In the states the Republicans made enormous gains in 1994, but, as discussed in Chapter 9, divided government remains at 1980s levels.

So, two years after some thought it had ended, the era of divided government is back. Even if the Republicans capture the presidency in 1996 while retaining control of Congress, or if Bill Clinton is reelected and the Democrats recapture Congress, the recent swings in party fortunes will make most commentators cautious about assuming that divided national government has ended, as some of them assumed too quickly in 1992. As for the states, the era of divided government continues uninterrupted.

The first edition of *Divided Government* concluded by taking note of James Sundquist's challenge to the profession. According to Sundquist, the old president-centered party government model had been replaced by a newer "coalition government" model, an unhappy development in his view, and political scientists had been remiss in not judging the comparative worth of the two models and communicating their views to the larger public. I demurred, suggesting that, not only were the alleged negative consequences of the new model far from proved, but even if they had been, a comparative judgment of the two models was impossible without an understanding of why voters had replaced the first with the second. In short, as political scientists, our first responsibility was research; judgment would come in due time.

In the short span of a few years, the profession has responded enthusiastically to Sundquist's challenge. That response, along with the intervening elections, is the occasion for this enlarged edition. One new chapter discusses the 1992 and 1994 election results at both the national level and in the states—a wealth of valuable new data. This chapter brings the material in Chapters 2 and 3 up to date. A second new chapter examines recent academic research on the possible causes of divided government discussed in Chapters 4 and 5. A third chapter considers what, if anything, the 1992–94 national experience tells us about divided government and reviews the conclusions of recent studies of the consequences of divided government. As in the first edition, much of the discussion in these new chapters is exploratory rather than conclusive. These are exciting times and we are only beginning to make sense of them.

***

A number of colleagues read and commented on the new chapters. For their help I thank James Alt, Keith Krehbiel and Paul Peterson.

In addition, I appreciate helpful comments from the following reviewers: Larry Dodd, University of Colorado; Sandy Maisel, Colby College; and David Mayhew, Yale University.

CHAPTER 1

INTRODUCTION

In 1988 George Bush led the Republicans to an impressive victory. Well, not exactly. While Bush was winning the presidency, carrying forty states with 54 percent of the popular vote, the Democrats were retaining their comfortable majorities in both houses of Congress, winning 260 of 435 House seats and 18 of 33 Senate seats. Politicians and pundits saw nothing unusual in this divided outcome. After all, Dwight Eisenhower's reelection in 1956 produced an identical division of our national institutions, as did Richard Nixon's election in 1968 and reelection in 1972. Moreover, Ronald Reagan's impressive victories in 1980 and 1984 failed to crack the Democratic House, though the Senate went the way of the presidency. Of the past six presidential elections, only one—1976—has given control of the presidency and both houses of Congress to one party. Judged against recent history, the 1988 outcome appeared to be more of the same, divided government as usual.

For political scientists, however, the 1988 outcome seemed to carry more weight. Even while observing year after year of divided government, we persisted in viewing it as something of an aberration, a departure from the "normal" condition of American politics. Of course, the exception seemed to have become the norm, but specific personalities and circumstances allowed us to disregard this continuing state of affairs. In 1956 a revered father figure, Eisenhower, was given a "personal" victory by an electorate still basically Democratic in its allegiance. In 1968 and 1972 Nixon triumphed over a Democratic party hopelessly split by the civil rights and antiwar movements. In 1980 Reagan didn't really win; rather, Jimmy Carter lost. And in 1984 the "great communicator" won a personal

1

victory reminiscent of Eisenhower's. Meanwhile, the seemingly overwhelming power of incumbency enabled Democratic majorities to control the Congress, or at least the House.

The 1988 outcome clearly exposed the limitations of such facile explanations. Democratic elites were as united as they had been since 1964 and highly optimistic about party prospects. The recent performance of the incumbent administration was not especially impressive. As for the personal appeal of George Bush, well, suffice it to say that the electorate did not see him as another Ronald Reagan or Dwight Eisenhower, or even a Mike Dukakis, for that matter.[1]

Against that background the election outcome drove home what academic studies had suggested for years, namely, that absent a truly major recession or costly war, it did not *matter* who won the Democratic and Republican presidential nominations; a generic Republican would defeat a generic Democrat.[2] Conversely, as scores of congressional elections researchers would testify, barring a national cataclysm the Republicans had no more chance of carrying the House than the proverbial snowball had of surviving the fires of hell.[3] Rather than an aberration produced by the accidental combination of particular circumstances and personalities, divided government has become a defining feature of contemporary American politics—it is the normal state of affairs.[4]

---

[1]Bush's leadership qualities were viewed as much inferior to Reagan's, though Bush fared better on dimensions such as integrity and competence. Contrary to the op-ed page consensus, the electorate regarded the personal qualities of Dukakis at least as favorably as those of Bush. See Herbert F. Weisberg, "Some Perspectives on the 1988 Presidential Election: The Roles of Turnout and Ronald Reagan," paper presented at the August, 1989 Annual Meetings of the American Political Science Association, Atlanta, GA: Table 5.

[2]Steven J. Rosenstone, *Forecasting Presidential Elections* (New Haven, CT: Yale University Press, 1983).

[3]Gary Jacobson, *The Electoral Origins of Divided Government* (Boulder, CO: Westview Press, 1990).

[4]In the early 1970s, some political scientists viewed divided government as a temporary condition marking the transition between the New Deal party system and an emerging Republican majority. By the 1980s, most analysts had come to doubt this view.

This realization produced a noticeable reaction among academics and commentators on public affairs. Sundquist, for example, condemned divided government, decrying its apparent inefficiency and irresponsibility.[5] The Committee on the Constitutional System (CCS), a blue-ribbon committee that had proposed constitutional changes designed to lessen the likelihood of divided government (among other things), was not ignored, as is the normal fate of blue-ribbon committees. Instead the CCS proposals provoked considerable debate that continues today.[6] Although most political scientists have not entered into such normatively charged arguments, more disinterested discussions of divided government are appearing in newer treatments of American government and politics.[7] With the realignment theme pretty much played out, divided government has the potential to become the new organizing principle of research in American politics in the 1990s.[8]

This book is an extended essay on divided government. Though it ranges rather broadly, three general concerns underlie the discussion. Reformers are most interested in the *consequences* of divided government for governing and policy-making, and this might *seem*

[5]James L. Sundquist, "Needed: A Political Theory for the New Era of Coalition Government in the United States," *Political Science Quarterly* 103 (1988): 613–35.

[6]See *A Bicentennial Analysis of the American Political Structure* (Washington, DC: Committee on the Constitutional System, 1987). Cf. Philip C. Bobbitt, "The Committee on the Constitutional System Proposals: Coherence and Dominance," *William and Mary Law Review* 30 (1989): 403–9; Erwin Chemerinsky, "The Question's Not Clear, but Party Government Is Not the Answer," *William and Mary Law Review* 30 (1989): 411–23; Mark A. Petracca, Lonce Bailey, and Pamela Smith, "Proposals for Constitutional Reform: An Evaluation of the Committee on the Constitutional System," *Presidential Studies Quarterly* 20 (1990): 503–32.

[7]See, for example, James A. Thurber, *Divided Democracy* (Washington, DC: CQ Press, 1991); Gary Cox and Samuel Kemell, eds., *The Politics of Divided Government* (Boulder, CO: Westview Press, 1991).

[8]On the growing skepticism about the realignment concept, see Everett Carll Ladd, "Like Waiting for Godot: The Uselessness of *Realignment* for Understanding Change in Contemporary American Politics," *Polity* 22 (1990): 511–25. On a suggested substitute for the realignment concept, see Byron E. Shafer, "The Notion of an Electoral Order: The Structure of Electoral Politics at the Accession of George Bush," in Byron E. Shafer, ed., *The End of Realignment* (Madison, WI: University of Wisconsin Press, 1991).

to be the question of most significance to citizens. Unfortunately, it is a question that has not received a great deal of academic attention, so the answers must be tentative. If that is so, why write this essay now, before more work is done? The answer is simply that some academics, commentators, and public figures already are sufficiently convinced of the harmful consequences of divided government that they seriously propose constitutional revision. To what extent does existing research—however incomplete—support such a strong recommendation?

The second underlying concern of this essay is more philosophical: whatever the actual consequences of divided government for governing and policy-making, a measured *evaluation* of those consequences requires that we consider what would happen if divided government were artificially ended via institutional reforms. Reformers are prone to compare an existing, imperfect state of affairs with some abstract, ideal standard. That is an important comparison; as a polity we should be cognizant of how far our politics falls short of the ideal. But the comparison that has more relevance for *actually* improving our politics is the comparison of what is to what would *likely be* if we changed it. It is simply not enough to identify negative consequences of divided government; it is necessary to show that those consequences are worse than those that would accompany proposed changes. With the best of intentions, we can "reform" one imperfect state into another even more imperfect.[9]

To evaluate the status quo we must compare it with the likely status quo after we intervene to "reform" it. That task brings us squarely to the third underlying question of this essay; why has the present status quo come to be? At this time in our history the Amer-

---

[9]Today's students typically are surprised to learn that the present PAC (political action committee) problem is largely a consequence of the campaign finance reform acts of the early 1970s. See Edwin Epstein, "Business and Labor Under the Federal Election Campaign Act of 1971," in Michael J. Malbin, ed., *Parties, Interest Groups, and Campaign Finance Laws* (Washington DC: American Enterprise Institute, 1980), 107–51. Similarly, many prominent critics of today's presidential nomination process trace their complaints back to repeated attempts to "reform" the process. For a discussion see Nelson Polsby, *Consequences of Party Reform* (New York: Oxford University Press, 1983).

ican electorate typically chooses to split control of our governing institutions between the parties. Why? This is the question that has been of most concern to academics, if not reformers, but it is anything but an "academic" question. *Only if we understand how we have gotten to where we are can we predict where we will go if we tinker with our institutions and political processes.* To put it more colloquially, if we fail to understand why divided government has come to be, we will have no one to blame if well-meaning reforms throw us out of the divided government frying pan into the unified government fire.

Thus, I will begin by putting the contemporary era into historical perspective; divided government is not new to our experience as a nation, but there are some respects in which the contemporary era is unique. Then I will augment the national perspective by considering developments in the American states; while largely unnoticed, their experience has paralleled the national experience. These discussions raise serious questions about two popular explanations of divided government; other explanations that appear more promising will be given further attention. With a better appreciation of how we have gotten to our present state, I then take up the question of the consequences of divided government and their implications for reform. Previewing that discussion, the bottom line of this essay is conservative, with a small *c.* To some degree, divided government in the United States probably reflects a lack of popular consensus about important issues, and a consequent unwillingness to trust either party with the full power to govern. If such sentiments were artificially restricted so as to force a choice between alternative unified governments, we would not necessarily benefit from a significantly more efficient and responsible government, and we might very well suffer other consequences that have not been sufficiently discussed. As I will argue, most of the world's democracies are governed by coalitions, a form of divided government; they are not obviously less well governed than we are.

CHAPTER 2

THE NATIONAL PICTURE

Historical Perspective

Divided government is nothing new in American history. Indeed, it might have appeared immediately after the Founding: Young and Riley argue that even during the one-party "Era of Good Feeling," when presidential candidates were nominated by the congressional caucus, government was effectively divided.[1] Leaving aside this ambiguous period, by 1832 the convention system of nominating presidential candidates had been established and two-party competition had been revived. Since that time national elections have created or continued a condition of divided government for 62 of 160 years, about 40 percent of our history (Table 2-1). The contemporary era (1952–92) stands out, with a majority (13/20) of presidential and mid-term elections producing divided governments, but other periods are unique in their own ways.[2] Consider the period encompassing the first half of the twentieth century. In those fifty-two years, twenty-two of twenty-six national elections resulted in *unified* control, something not matched either before or after. There is some irony here in that historical accounts contrast the highly organized nineteenth-century parties and their fiercely partisan members with

[1]James Sterling Young and Russell L. Riley, "Party Government and Political Culture," paper presented at the September, 1990 Annual Meetings of the American Political Science Association, San Francisco (in press).
[2]For purposes of this essay, we will date the contemporary era as having begun in 1952. Although two years of unified Republican control followed that election, in retrospect, it was the end of New Deal Democratic hegemony.

Table 2-1   Control of National Institutions, 1832–1992

	Unified	Divided
1832–1992	49[a]	31
1832–1900	20	14
1900–1952	22	4
1952–1992	7	13

[a]Number of elections
Source: Tabulated from *Members of Congress Since 1789* (Washington, DC: Congressional Quarterly Inc., 1985), 182–83.

the less well organized and militant twentieth-century parties.[3] The regional realignment of the 1890s, the Progressive movement, and the rapid social and economic transformation of the country all combined to weaken the parties' capacity to structure the electoral process—to control nominations, to deliver the vote, and to organize office-holders.[4] All of this suggests a general decline in party influence in American politics. And yet, a macro-level indicator of the parties' ability to structure American politics—unified control—shows the opposite movement. Progressive reforms might have weakened the parties at the turn of the century, but that weakening did not translate into divided control. Rather, the Republicans dominated the first quarter of the century (with a Wilsonian interregnum), while the second quarter saw the Democrats dominate. In

[3]For a wide-ranging account of partisan politics in the North after the Civil War, and its decline after the turn of the century, see Michael E. McGerr, *The Decline of Popular Politics* (New York: Oxford, 1986).
[4]For overviews see Everett Carll Ladd, Jr., American Political Parties (New York: Norton, 1970), chap. 4; James L. Sundquist, *Dynamics of the Party System*, rev. ed. (Washington, DC: Brookings, 1983), chaps. 7–8; and Joel H. Silbey, "The Rise and Fall of American Political Parties, 1790–1990," in L. Sandy Maisel, ed., *The Parties Respond* (Boulder, CO: Westview Press, 1990), 3–17.

neither case was there much in the way of divided control.[5] All in all, the contemporary period is more of a departure from the earlier twentieth-century pattern than it is from American history in general.

This background makes it easy to understand the frustration with contemporary divided government expressed by Sundquist's generation of scholars. As he observes, the textbook account of the operation of modern American politics is a version of responsible party theory that posits strong presidential leadership of a cohesive majority party. A generation whose formative experiences lay in the first half of the twentieth century might understandably regard such an account as not only factually accurate but also normatively good— the period included forty-four years of unified control, and the presidencies of Theodore Roosevelt, Woodrow Wilson, and Franklin Roosevelt covered twenty-eight of those forty-four years. During this period the country successfully fought two world wars and weathered the greatest economic crisis in our history, all of which would seem to provide a *prima facie* case for taking seriously the argument that American institutions function best under unified control.

Yet a closer look at the historical record provides another, more conditional, perspective. Divided government clearly tends to characterize those times identified by political historians as periods of chronic societal strain (Table 2-2). All of the divided government that occurred in the nineteenth century occurred in the periods 1840–60 and 1874–96. In the first period, abolitionism and nativism cross-cut the parties. The period ended with the elections of 1860, which brought unified Republican control and civil war. Fourteen years of unified Republican control came to an end when the Southern Democrats returned to Congress in 1874. The next two decades rank with the contemporary period in their frequency of divided control. The rapid pace of economic development thrust what had heretofore been local issues into state and national arenas, and the

---

[5]The four elections that divided control were all mid-terms. The administration lost Congress at the conclusion of each of the world wars—1918 and 1946. The Republicans lost the House in 1910 (concurrently with the party split that led to the three-way election of 1912 that put Wilson in the White House). They lost the House again in 1930 following the Great Crash.

Table 2-2 Major Periods of Divided Government

	Unified	Divided
1840–60	4[a]	6
1874–96	3	8
1952–92	7	13
Three-period total	14	27
All other	35	4

[a]Number of elections

Source: Tabulated from *Members of Congress Since 1789* (Washington, DC: Congressional Quarterly Inc., 1985), 182–83.

parties' mass bases were rent by ethno-cultural divisions.[6] What has been called the "period of indecision" came to an end only with the depression and sectional realignment of the 1890s and fourteen years of unified Republican rule.[7]

Seen against this background, our times appear less exceptional. The Viet Nam War, the complex of concerns known as the social issue, and especially race buffeted the New Deal party system much as slavery, industrialization, and wars buffeted earlier party systems, with similar results for control of national institutions.[8] In the past, as well as now, intractable problems and/or irresolvable differences have not been conducive to unified control. As a discipline, political

[6]Paul Kleppner, *The Third Electoral System, 1853–1892: Parties, Voters, and Political Cultures* (Chapel Hill, NC: University of North Carolina Press, 1979).

[7]To fully appreciate the phrase "period of indecision," consider that in the five presidential elections between 1876 and 1892, no candidate won as much as 51 percent of the popular vote, four won with less than 50 percent (because of the presence of small third parties), and two plurality losers (1876, 1888) were victorious in the electoral college. With such knife-edge results in the presidential races, it is not surprising that off-year congressional outcomes often went against the presidential winner.

[8]On the pervasive effects of race, see Edward G. Carmines and James A. Stimson, *Race and the Transformation of American Politics* (Princeton, NJ: Princeton University Press, 1989).

science has paid considerable attention to the unified governments that dealt with major problems that precipitated realignments.[9] Secession, the crash of the 1890s, and the Great Depression—all were "dealt with" by fourteen years of unified control. We have paid less attention to the fact that in two of three cases the periods leading up to such calamities were characterized by divided control.

This observation immediately raises the chicken-or-egg problem: which comes first, political failure or divided control? Notice that "great presidencies" do not appear in eras of divided government. Harrison, Tyler, Polk, Taylor, Fillmore, Pierce, and Buchanan do not make any historian's top five list, nor do Grant, Hayes, Cleveland, and Arthur. The jury is still out on the presidents of the contemporary era, but it seems safe to guess that there are no Washingtons or Lincolns in the bunch, nor probably any FDRs. Were the men who served in eras of divided government all personally weak and ineffectual, or did divided control prevent them from realizing their potential? Would FDR have been as great if he had faced opposition majorities in the House throughout his presidency, as contemporary Republican presidents do? Would Buchanan have been as weak if he had had a dependable majority in Congress? No one can provide persuasive answers to such counterfactual questions, but the correlation between chronic problems, weak presidencies, and divided control suggests consideration of more than one causal scenario. Rather than blithely assume that division of control and weak presidencies cause social and economic breakdowns, we should at least consider the possibility that social and economic problems cause division of control *and* weak presidencies. If the latter is the case, then some of today's reformers have the situation "bass ackwards."

Understanding National Divided Government

Thus far I have emphasized the nonuniqueness of contemporary politics, but there is one important respect in which the contemporary period actually is unique. In the present era, divided control has been as likely to accompany presidential elections as mid-terms: six

[9]David W Brady, *Critical Elections and Congressional Policy Making* (Stanford, CA: Stanford University Press, 1988).

Table 2-3 Divided Government by Type of
Election

	Presidential	Mid-term
1832–1992	9	22
1832–1900	3	11
1900–1952	0	4
1952–92	6	7
1840–60	1	5
1874–96	2	6
1952–92	6	7
Other	0	4

Source: Tabulated from *Members of Congress Since 1789*
(Washington, DC: Congressional Quarterly Inc., 1985),
182–83.

of the former and seven of the latter resulted in split control (Table
2-3). In earlier times, however, divided control virtually always was
the result of a mid-term loss of unified control achieved in the preceding presidential election. Between 1832 and 1952 only three of
eighteen elections that resulted in divided government were in presidential years, and each is arguably special. The 1848 election was a
three-way race in which a former Democratic president, Martin Van
Buren, ran on the Free Soil ticket, throwing the presidency to the
Whigs.[10] In 1876 the Democrats carried the House and the *popular*
vote for president, while the Republicans won the *electoral* vote and
the Senate.[11] In 1884, the partially insulated Senate again held out
against the victorious Democrats. Before Eisenhower's reelection in

[10]Van Buren took 10 percent of the national vote and received 25 percent or more in
a number of large northern states such as New York and Massachusetts.
[11]A special electoral commission awarded three disputed Southern states to the
Republicans, giving Rutherford Hayes an electoral vote majority. In return for not
blocking the commission recommendation, Southern Democrats in the House of
Representatives got the end of Reconstruction and aid in rebuilding the South's
infrastructure.

1956, winners of two-way presidential races had *always* carried the House, and only in 1884 had one failed to carry the Senate.[12]

Thus, explanations of divided government in the nineteenth century should focus on asymmetric patterns of defection and turnout in mid-term elections, whereas explanations of divided government in the contemporary period should focus at least as much, and probably more, on split-ticket voting. Not since 1954 has a mid-term *begun* a period of divided government; in the contemporary period, six other mid-terms *continued* a divided condition that had been established by ticket-splitting in the preceding presidential election.[13]

The underpinnings of contemporary divided government appear in Table 2-4. We do not have data on presidential voting within congressional districts in the nineteenth century, but as suggested by the figures of the early 1900s, it was probably quite unusual for a district to cast a majority of its presidential votes for one party and a majority of its congressional votes for the other.[14] In recent years, however, 40 percent of all districts have reported such split verdicts. Since national survey data became available in the 1950s, we can probe beneath the aggregate figures to determine the rates of individual ticket-splitting. Between the 1950s, and 1980s,

---

[12]Interestingly, the unprecedented nature of the 1956 outcome appears to have escaped academic notice. Consider *The American Voter* (Angus Campbell, Philip Converse, Warren Miller, and Donald Stokes, New York: Wiley, 1960), a path-breaking work whose arguments and ideas dominated the study of voting behavior for the better part of two decades. Based largely on survey data from the 1956 election, the book mentions the congressional outcome only in passing and nowhere recognizes that 1956 was the first time in history that a president elected in a two-way race failed to carry either chamber of Congress.

[13]Similarly, Alford and Hibbing find that prior to World War II, mid-term elections accurately predicted the winner of the next presidential election. Obviously, that is not true in the contemporary era. John Alford and John Hibbing, "The Demise of the Upper House and the Rise of the Senate: Electoral Responsiveness in the United States Senate," presented at the August, 1987 Annual Meetings of the American Political Science Association, Washington, DC.

[14]Historians generally agree that split-ticket voting was rare. Even if voters were so inclined, splitting a ticket was difficult. Prior to the Australian ballot reforms, the parties printed their own ballots, generally using different colors and listing only their own nominees. Thus, a voter who wished to split often had to cross out names, combine two ballots, and do so publicly. See Jerrold Rusk, "The Effect of the Australian Ballot Reform on Split Ticket Voting: 1876–1908," *American Political Science Review*, 64 (1970):1220–38.

Table 2-4   Percentage of Congressional Districts Carried by
House and Presidential Candidates of Different Parties

Year	Percentage	Year	Percentage	Year	Percentage
1900	3	1948	21	1972	44
1908	7	1952	19	1976	29
1916	11	1956	30	1980	33
1924	12	1960	26	1984	45
1932	14	1964	33	1988	34
1940	15	1968	32		

Source: Adapted from Norman Ornstein, Thomas Mann, and Michael Malbin, *Vital Statistics on Congress, 1989–1990* (Washington, DC: Congressional Quarterly Inc., 1990), Table 2.14.

ticket-splitting almost doubled, from 15 percent or less of the electorate to 25 percent or more. The largest jump occurred between 1964 and 1972, the so-called time of troubles, with no apparent increase since then (Figure 2-1).

In a period of party decomposition, it is not surprising that ticket-splitting should increase.[15] The weakening of party bonds makes voters more likely to respond to attractive candidates and issues of the other party. But contemporary ticket-splitting is not random; rather, it follows a pattern that must be accounted for by a complete explanation of the behavior: the observed splitting favors Republican presidents and Democratic representatives by a noticeable margin over Democratic presidents and Republican representatives (Table 2-5). The asymmetry obviously is most pronounced in the Republican landslides of 1956, 1972, and 1984, and until 1972 Republican weakness in the South artificially enhanced the national pattern. But the asymmetry is a relatively consistent feature of national elections in the contemporary era. Thus, proposed explanations of divided national government must explain (1) why split-ticket voting increased sharply between the mid-1960s and mid-1970s and (2) why split-ticket voting favors Republican presidents

[15]Indeed, ticket-splitting has generally been viewed as an indicator of party decomposition. See Walter Dean Burnham, *Critical Elections and the Mainsprings of American Politics* (New York: Norton, 1970); 106–20.

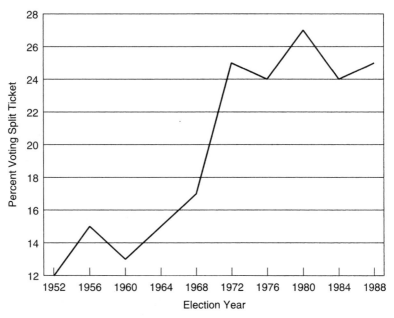

Figure 2-1 Split-Ticket Voting for President and U.S. Representatives

and Democratic representatives. The two most popular explanations of divided national government founder on these simple criteria.

Two Common Explanations for Divided National Government

Gerrymandering and incumbency are the two most commonly offered explanations for the contemporary state of divided national government. Do they pass the simple explanatory criteria suggested above? In the case of gerrymandering, at least, the answer is clearly no.

Gerrymandering

Republicans understandably have been frustrated by recent national election outcomes. Since 1968 they have lost only two presidential

Table 2-5 Patterns of President–House Ticket-Splitting

Year	Whole Country		Non-South	
	Dem. Pres. Rep. House	Rep. Pres. Dem. House	Dem. Pres. Rep. House	Rep. Pres. Dem. House
	%	%	%	%
1952	2	10	3	5
1956	2	14	3	11
1960	4	10	6	7
1964	9	6	10	5
1968[a]	7	11	7	9
1972	5	25	5	20
1976	9	15	10	13
1980[a]	9	18	10	16
1984	6	18	5	17
1988	7	18	7	16

[a]Excludes Wallace/Anderson voters.
Source: American National Election Studies (ANES).

elections (1976, and that, in the aftermath of the Watergate scandal, by less than 1 percent, to a Southern evangelical), and 1992. They may understandably believe that they "own" the contemporary presidency. In addition, Republicans captured the Senate in 1980 and held it through the 1984 elections, and most observers believe that the Senate remains competitive today. But the House of Representatives is another matter. Even as Republican presidential candidates sweep the country (forty-one states in 1984), Democratic majorities in the House persisted almost unaffected until 1994, thorns in the sides of Republican presidents.

Contemplating their lack of success in the House, some Republicans have focused on gerrymandering as the cause of their troubles. Given Democratic strength at the state legislative level, where the congressional lines generally are drawn, it is understandable that

Republicans should suspect skullduggery in the districting process. Some well-publicized and unarguable gerrymanders such as the Burton heist in California add support to their suspicions.[16]

As it turns out, however, researchers who have carefully studied the question are unanimous in discounting the contribution of gerrymandering to divided government.[17] Effects in particular states are identifiable, to be sure, but the *net* effects are slight—most of what Burton stole in California the Republicans stole back in Indiana and other states. Moreover, gerrymanders show a notable lack of persistence.[18] It seems that a few examples, however striking, do not add up to a national pattern.

But it is the rise in split-ticket voting that eviscerates the gerrymandering argument. That argument implicitly assumes that Republican House candidates receive as many votes as presidential candidates, but they do not win a fair proportion of seats because their votes are "wasted" by Democratic gerrymanders. The flaw in the argument is obvious. The Republicans' basic problem in House races is that they do not get as many *votes* as their presidential candidates. In 1984, for example, Ronald Reagan received almost 57 percent of the national vote, but his partisan associates in House races received only 47 percent. Republicans failed to capture the House not because they were cheated by Democratic gerrymanderers; rather, they did not capture a majority in the House because on balance *seventeen million* more voters preferred Reagan to Mondale than preferred Republican congressional candidates to Democrats. *Not since 1952 have Republican House candidates received more votes in total than Democratic candidates.* Thus, Republicans have no beef with the nation's districting arrangements. They *do not* win a majority of House seats but they *should not* win a majority of House seats because they do not receive a majority of House votes.

At this point some Republicans might object that although they do not win majorities of House votes, their proportion of House

[16]The late Representative Philip Burton drew a plan that was widely credited with transforming a Democratic edge of 22–21 into a wide lead of 28–17.
[17]See the discussion in Thomas Mann, "Is the House of Representatives Unresponsive to Political Change?" in A. James Reichley, ed., *Elections American Style* (Washington, DC: Brookings, 1987), 269–76.
[18]While the Indiana Republicans turned a 6–5 Democratic lead in 1980 into a 4–6 lag in 1982, by 1990 the Democrats again led 8–2.

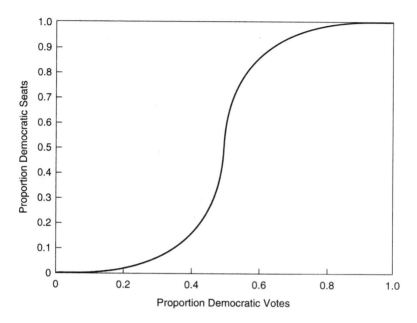

Figure 2-2 The Relationship between Seats and Votes in Two-Party Single-Member District Systems

seats never is as high as the proportion of the vote they do receive—surely a reflection of some chicanery in the process of drawing lines. The fact is correct; the interpretation is not. In *all* single-member district electoral systems, the party that receives fewer votes receives a less than proportional seat total.[19] That is, the relation between seats and votes is not linear, but S-shaped (Figure 2-2). Below 50 percent of the national vote, a party receives a smaller proportion of the seats; above 50 percent, the party receives a larger proportion of seats.[20] Thus, in 1984 the Republicans won 47 percent of the aggre-

---

[19]Such systems are characteristic of Anglo-American democracies. The nation is divided into numerous geographic divisions (congressional districts in the United States), and in each division's election the winner takes all.

[20]In many existing systems (and formerly in the United States) a 1 percent increase in vote in the 40 to 50 percent interval yields a 3 percent or higher increase in seats—the rationale for the so-called cube law of elections. For a discussion see Gary King and Robert X. Browning, "Democratic Representation and Partisan Bias in Congressional Elections," *American Political Science Review* 81 (1987); 1251–73.

gate House vote, but only 42 percent of the seats. In a sense, they *were* cheated, but by the electoral system—not by Democratic gerrymanders. Had the Republicans won a majority of votes, the normal operation of the electoral system in all likelihood would have "cheated" the Democrats.

The abstract seats–votes curve in Figure 2-2 is "unbiased" in the sense that it is symmetric and passes through the point (50, 50) where 50 percent of the vote results in 50 percent of the seats. If the curve is shifted to one side, the system is biased in the sense that one party wins a larger proportion of seats with a given percentage of the vote than the other party wins with the same percentage. Ironically, the most detailed research finds that the post-war American electoral system is biased in favor of the *Republicans*. King and Gelman show that controlling for incumbency, the Republicans can expect to win more seats with a given vote percentage than can the Democrats with an identical vote percentage.[21] Basically, the greater geographic concentration of Democratic voters in urban areas makes it more likely that their votes will be wasted in excess majorities for Democratic candidates. There is, to be sure, a kicker in the King–Gelman finding; namely, "controlling for incumbency."

Incumbency

Reflecting on the 1984 elections, columnist William Schneider wrote:

> It was incumbency that saved the Democratic Party from ruin. If the government had passed a decree prohibiting incumbents from running for reelection, the Republican Party would probably have gained control of both Houses of Congress and a substantial number of statehouses.[22]

If asked about divided national government, the advantage of incumbency is certainly the first explanation most political scientists would offer. There is a huge literature on this subject, far too much

---

[21]Gary King and Andrew Gelman, "Systemic Consequences of Incumbency Advantage in U.S. House Elections," *American Journal of Political Science* 35 (1991): 110–38.
[22]"Half a Realignment," *The New Republic* 191 (3 December 1984): 20.

to review here.[23] Summarizing briefly, in the mid-1960s the margins by which House incumbents won reelection drifted upward. Statistical estimates placed the pre-1964 advantage at 1 or 2 percent, and the post-1964 advantage at 5 percent, increasing to 8 or 9 percent in the 1970s.[24] Already enjoying reelection rates in the neighborhood of 90 percent a generation ago, today's House incumbents have been winning at rates of 96–98 percent. The improved electoral showings of our representatives have a number of causes. They receive tax-payer-funded perks that have an estimated value of as much as one million dollars per year.[25] The expanded role of government enables them to earn voter gratitude by providing various nonpartisan and nonprogrammatic constituency services.[26] More recently, the campaign financing advantage of incumbents has become overwhelming. Whatever the relative contribution of various factors, it is undeniable that it is difficult to defeat a member of the contemporary House of Representatives.[27]

Increased margins of victory led to a decline in the number of marginal districts, and thus a decline in the number of outcomes that would be determined by a president's "coattails."[28] Consequently, even without an increase in split-ticket voting, the distribution of House seats would have become less responsive to variations in the

---

[23]For a recent survey of the development of congressional careers, see Morris P. Fiorina and Timothy Prinz, "Legislative Incumbency and Insulation," in Joel H. Silbey, ed., *Encyclopedia of the American Legislative System* (New York: Charles Scribner's Sons, 1992).

[24]Gelman and King argue that even these estimates are biased downward and that the true incumbency advantage is in the neighborhood of 12 percent. See their "Systemic Consequences."

[25]Specifically, such perks include personal staffs that currently average seventeen per member; multiple district offices; and essentially unlimited travel, franked mail, and audio-visual support. See Norman J. Ornstein, Thomas E. Mann, and Michael J. Malbin, *Vital Statistics on Congress 1989–1990* (Washington, DC: Congressional Quarterly Inc., 1990), chap. 5.

[26]Morris P. Fiorina, *Congress—Keystone of the Washington Establishment*, 2nd ed. (New Haven, CT: Yale University Press, 1989).

[27]One should not assume, however (with some supporters of term limitations), that contemporary incumbents are lazy and unresponsive. In fact, they seem to work very hard to achieve their high reelection rates and take nothing for granted. See Chapter 4.

[28]David R. Mayhew, "Congressional Elections: The Case of the Vanishing Marginals," *Polity* 6 (1974): 295–317.

presidential vote.[29] Increased ticket-splitting lessens that responsiveness still more. Thus, Republican presidential victories in the
contemporary era have not had the payoffs in House seats that were
common even a generation ago.

How does incumbency explain the *pattern* of ticket-splitting?
This is less clear. Historical accident may be part of the answer. The
Democrats were the House majority in the mid-1960s when the
electorate's party affiliations began to weaken, when the role of government expanded, and when new technologies (polling, direct mail,
computers) began to affect congressional elections. So, even if both
parties were equally likely to adapt to new opportunities, there were
more Democrats to make the adaptation than Republicans. Of
course, this argument has the counter-factual implication that if the
Republicans had been the House majority during the mid-1960s, we
would now be living in a unified Republican era.

Most observers find such a counter-factual dubious, suggesting
that something more is needed to complete the explanation. Alan
Ehrenhalt argues that Democrats and Republicans were *not* equally
likely to adapt to the new style of politics.[30] Believing in a minimal
government role and opposing the existence of many government
programs, Republican representatives are personally less willing to
perform the kind of constituency nurturing that is a major component of the incumbency advantage. They also are less likely to seek
to expand government for the benefit of their districts. In short,
Democratic ideology fits the congressional times better than Republican.[31] Against this argument stands research showing that Republi-

[29]There is some controversy about this point. For alternative points of view, see Gary
Jacobson, "The Marginals Never Vanished: Incumbency and Competition in
Elections to the U.S. House of Representatives," *American Journal of Political Science*
31 (1987): 126–41. Steven Ansolabehere, David W. Brady, and Morris P. Fiorina,
"The Marginals Never Vanished?" *British Journal of Political Science* (January 1992):
121–138.

[30]"Why a Pay Raise Would Be Good for the GOP," *Congressional Quarterly Weekly
Report*, (31 December 1982): 3175.

[31]Ehrenhalt carries the argument a step further, arguing that the personal quality of
Democratic candidates exceeds that of Republicans because Democratic candidates
like government and the prospect of using it, whereas some qualified Republican
candidates opt out rather than engage in activities they oppose. *The United States of
Ambition* (New York: Times Books, 1991), passim.

can incumbents have no less of an electoral advantage than Democrats.[32]

So, while some subsidiary links in the argument are problematic, on the whole incumbency appears to offer a plausible explanation for the current condition of divided national control. According to this explanation, divided government is something of an accident. On the basis of performance and issues, the contemporary electorate favors Republican presidential candidates. But House elections are affected less by national conditions and issues and more by the personal qualities and activities of the candidates. The Democratic majorities that were in place during the early 1960s have used the advantage of incumbency to retain office by inducing constituents to split their tickets when they support Republican presidential candidates.

Neat. Probably too neat. Certainly House incumbency is an important element of divided national government. If the relation between seats and votes had stayed constant at 1950s' levels, it is likely that the Republicans would have captured the House in 1972 and 1984, although they would have done so with a minority of the vote, reflecting the King–Gelman finding that the underlying system is biased in their favor.[33] Yet experts on congressional elections have raised doubts about the sufficiency of the incumbency explanation of divided government. Parts of the overall picture, especially election outcomes in open seats, simply are not explained by incumbency.

One of the foremost students of congressional elections, Gary Jacobson, asserts that

> Undeniably, incumbency confers considerable advantages, but it cannot explain why Democrats defeated enough Republicans to regain control of the Senate (or why they lost it in the first place). It cannot explain why a larger proportion of Republican representatives (4.7 percent) than Democratic representatives (3.7 percent) have been defeated in the last five general elections. Nor can it explain why Republicans have not won more open seats.[34]

---

[32]King and Gelman, "Systemic Consequences."

[33]See the illustrative calculations in Ansolabehere, Brady, and Fiorina, "The Marginals Never Vanished?"

[34]"Congress: A Singular Continuity," in Michael Nelson, ed., *The Elections of 1988* (Washington, DC: CQ Press, 1989): 143.

Jacobson's final observation is critical. Elsewhere he reports that during the period of Republican presidential dominance—Nixon's election in 1968 to Bush's election in 1988—only twenty-eight House seats have *not* come open.[35] In other words, 94 percent of all House seats have been open at some time during the era that Republican presidential candidates were rolling over their Democratic opponents. How did the Republicans do in all of these open seat races, where, by definition, incumbency was not operative? The answer, Jacobson reports, is that they made a net gain of two seats! The Democrats had roughly a 60–40 edge in the late 1960s, and they retain that edge today.

A little reflection aided by a little algebra reveals the full significance of this finding. Suppose that all seats in an election are open. Let *d* denote the probability that the Democrats retain a seat they presently hold and *r* denote the corresponding Republican probability. Then $(1 - d)$ denotes the probability the Republicans capture a Democratic seat, and $(1 - r)$ the probability the Democrats capture a Republican seat. In order for an existing Democrat:Republican ratio of 60:40 to hold after the election, the following equation must hold:[36]

$$\frac{60}{40} = \frac{60d + 40\,(1 - r)}{40r + 60\,(1 - d)}$$

which requires that $r = 1.5d - .5$. An examination of this equation shows that when *r* and *d* are both greater than .5 (each party on average has better than an even chance of retaining a seat it presently holds), *d* must be greater than *r*. That is, *to preserve its majority, the Democrats must have a systematically higher probability of retaining their seats than the Republicans, even though all seats are open by assumption.* This is a simplified model, to be sure, and House seats do not come open simultaneously, as supposed here, but consistent with the

[35] *The Electoral Origins of Divided Government* (Boulder, CO: Westview Press, 1990), 32–7.
[36] To explain, the proportion of existing seats held by Democrats (60 percent) must equal the percentage of seats retained (60 percent times *d*) plus the percentage taken from the Republicans (40 percent times $1 - r$). Analogously, for Republicans, existing seats (40 percent) must equal the percentage retained (40 percent times *r*) plus the percentage taken from Democrats (60 percent times $1 - d$).

model, Jacobson reports that over the 1968–1990 period the probability that the Democrats retained an open seat was .80, while the analogous Republican probability was only .72. Stated differently, over the past generation the Republicans have had about two chances in ten of taking an open seat from the Democrats, but the Democrats have had almost three chances in ten of taking one from the Republicans. Relatively speaking, the flip of the electoral coin in open seats is almost 50 percent more favorable to the Democrats.

Why? There are a number of possible explanations for this additional pro-Democratic force. Some believe that the Republican disadvantage in House elections arises from the simple fact that the country is fundamentally Democratic on the issues, as suggested by continued Democratic success in state and local elections. Only a presidential nomination process that gives undue influence and visibility to unpopular constituency groups allows the Republicans to win the highest office. Thus, the apparent Republican disadvantage in House elections is actually a Democratic disadvantage in presidential elections. Alternatively, Jacobson argues that voters regard Republicans as the party of peace and prosperity and Democrats as the party of ordinary people. Thus, Republican presidents and Democratic congresses maximize the fit between party and institutional strengths.[37] Elsewhere I have suggested that ticket-splitting enables voters to register a preference for a middle-of-the-road outcome when the two parties persist in offering them extremes.[38]

By and by we will consider these other explanations, but let us leave the question open for now. For present purposes what is important is that even after incumbency is removed from the picture, a Democratic advantage in House elections remains. Explanations of divided government based on incumbency must be supplemented with other explanations that identify additional considerations favorable to House Democrats. Before searching for these other explanations, let us seek some broader perspective by considering the experience of the American states.

---

[37] *Electoral Origins of Divided Government*, 112–20.
[38] "The Reagan Years: Turning to the Right or Groping Toward the Middle," in Barry Cooper, Allan Kornberg, and William Mishler, eds., *The Resurgence of Conservatism in Anglo-American Democracies* (Durham, NC: Duke University Press, 1988), 430–59.

THE STATES

Divided government has been defined and discussed primarily in national terms: the Republicans consistently win the presidency while the Democrats win Congress, or at least the House of Representatives. This national emphasis is understandable enough. While the role of the states should not be disparaged, as a practical matter the national government is much more important than the governments of the states. Consequently, national politics dominates the perspective of contemporary political discussion.

But developments in the states merit our attention. In retrospect it appears that the contemporary era of divided national government began with the first Eisenhower election in 1952, solidified when Nixon emerged as the choice of a badly split electorate in 1968, and became the norm by the 1980s. Although little noticed, developments in the states have been somewhat similar. Unified control in the states declined sharply after the 1952 elections, stabilized at a lower level in the late 1960s, and declined still further in the 1980s (Figure 3-1).[1] These developments are interesting in themselves, but

---

[1]Divided government exists whenever the governor and both houses of the legislature are not controlled by the same party (states with nonpartisan legislatures—Nebraska, and Minnesota before 1972—are omitted from the tabulations). The reported figures indicate the presence or absence of unified government following the state elections of that year (or the preceding year in states holding elections in odd-numbered years), *but the number of states that actually elected both governor and legislatures in that year varies.* That is, in 1952 thirty-two states held gubernatorial elections in presidential election years. This number fell to twelve by 1966 and remains at twelve today. Also, during the period under study, twenty states extended the terms of their governors and some extended legislative terms as well.

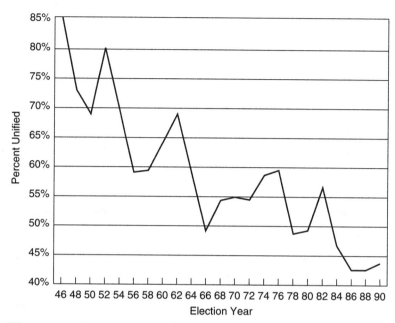

Figure 3-1   Unified State Governments

they have important implications for discussions of divided national government as well. Discussions of presidential-congressional splits naturally emphasize national-level factors—House incumbency, the Democratic presidential nomination process, and so forth. But trends in state elections parallel to those in national elections raise suspicions that more general forces are at work and that existing explanations of divided government are too level-specific. Put somewhat strongly, whatever the disparity in practical importance, from the standpoint of democratic theory each state's experience is as interesting as that of the nation. The states share the larger cultural context, and have similar institutional structures and political processes. The national experience is but one observation among fifty-one—from a scientific standpoint a case study, although one of great interest and importance.

I will begin by noting the striking disassociation of recent state legislative and gubernatorial outcomes. Then I will describe the patterns of party control in the American states since World War II.

This survey identifies a number of questions that encourage us to think more generally about the entire subject of divided government.

The Illusion of Democratic Dominance in State Elections

Election post-mortems in the 1980s regularly emphasized the "shallowness" of Republican victories. Not only did the Republicans fail to crack the House of Representatives, in state elections the Democrats typically captured more than 60 percent of the governorships and legislative seats. Such outcomes leave a natural impression of Democratic dominance of state government. Commenting on the 1984 elections, for example, Chubb and Peterson remark that "a sizable majority of state governments remain solidly Democratic."[2] In fact, such impressions of Democratic dominance of state governments are mistaken. As Burnham observes, after the 1988 elections almost three-quarters of the American population lived in divided states.[3] A complete tabulation reveals that Democrats have controlled a majority of state governments for only six years since World War II—the two years following their landslide presidential victory of 1964 and the four years following the 1974 Republican debacle. How does this fact square with the 60+ percent success levels in state elections? The answer is that Democratic successes in gubernatorial and legislative elections have become decoupled to a truly remarkable degree.

Table 3-1 charts patterns of party control following the 1978, 1982, and 1986 elections (three-quarters of the states hold their gubernatorial elections in the off-years). The Democratic party held 63 percent of the legislatures and 62 percent of the governorships after these three elections. Now, if party success in one arena had absolutely nothing to do with party success in the other, one could construct the expected distribution of unified and divided governments by simply multiplying the respective marginal probabilities of party control. Of

---

[2]John E. Chubb and Paul E. Peterson, "Realignment and Institutionalization," in Chubb and Peterson, eds., *The New Direction in American Politics* (Washington, DC: Brookings, 1985), 2.
[3]Walter Dean Burnham, "The Reagan Heritage," in Gerald M. Pomper, ed., *The Election of 1988* (Chatham, NJ: Chatham House Publishers, 1989), 20.

Table 3-1 Gubernatorial and Legislative
Victories: 1978, 1982, 1986

Governors	No.	Proportion
Democratic	90	.62
Republican	56	.38

Legislatures		
Democratic	93	.63
Republican	33	.22
Split	21	.14

Patterns of State Government Control

	No.	Proportion	Expected proportion
Unified Democratic	58	.40	.40
Unified Republican	14	.10	.08
Divided: Democratic governor	32	.22	.22
Divided: Republican governor	42	.29	.30

Source: Calculated from *Statistical Abstract of the United States.* Washington, DC: U.S. Government Printing Office.

course, such a baseline model would strike most analysts as ridiculous, but as Table 3-1 shows, legislative and gubernatorial control in fact appear to be completely independent: whether a party holds the executive has nothing to do with the likelihood that it holds the legislature.[4] Consequently, although the Democrats do win more than 60 percent of the governor's races and a similar number of state legislatures, they *control* only 40 percent of the state governments.[5]

[4]Applying a chi-square test for independence, $p > .99$.
[5]Jacobson points out that House election results have also become increasingly independent of gubernatorial and state legislative elections. Gary Jacobson, *The Electoral Origins of Divided Government* (Boulder, CO: Westwood Press, 1990), chap. 2.

Divided Government

This noteworthy disassociation between gubernatorial and legislative control has existed for some time. Table 3-2 replicates Table 3-1 for the 1962, 1966, and 1970 elections. Again, there is no significant relationship between party control in the two arenas. Not until we go back to the 1950s do we find some semblance of a party-based relationship between gubernatorial and legislative control (Table 3-3). A generation ago, even with pluralities of the governorships and legislatures in opposite party hands, there

Table 3-2   Gubernatorial and Legislative Victories: 1962, 1966, 1970

Governors	No.	Proportion
Democratic	81	.58
Republican	59	.42

Legislatures		
Democratic	72	.51
Republican	51	.36
Split	17	.12

Patterns of State Government Control

	No.	Proportion	Expected proportion
Unified Democratic	51	.36	.30
Unified Republican	30	.21	.15
Divided: Democratic governor	30	.21	.28
Divided: Republican governor	29	.21	.26

Source: Calculated from *Statistical Abstract of the United States.* Washington, DC: U.S. Government Printing Office.

Table 3-3   Gubernatorial and Legislative
              Victories: 1948, 1952, 1956

Governors	No.	Proportion
Democratic	72	.54
Republican	61	.46

Legislatures		
Democratic	56	.42
Republican	59	.44
Split	18	.14

Patterns of State Government Control

	No.	Proportion	Expected proportion
Unified Democratic	48	.36	.23
Unified Republican	47	.35	.20
Divided: Democratic governor	24	.18	.31
Divided: Republican governor	14	.11	.26

Source: Calculated from *Statistical Abstract of the United States.* Washington, DC: U.S. Government Printing Office.

was a significant relationship between party control in the two arenas.[6]

Findings such as these generally are discussed under the heading of "party decomposition."[7] Certainly, party is less a unifying force in

[6]Applying a chi-square test, $p < .01$. Because most of the states held gubernatorial elections in presidential years in the early 1950s, this comparison is based on three presidential year elections (see footnote 1).

[7]Clubb, Flanigan, and Zingale discuss declines in unified state government as aspects of the party decomposition phase of realignments. See Jerome M. Clubb, William H. Flanigan, and Nancy H. Zingale, *Partisan Realignment* (Boulder: Westview Press, 1990), chap. 6.

the behavior of voters now than it was a generation ago, but such an observation takes us only so far. Party decline allows other factors to work, but does not in itself determine those factors or explain their operation. At the national level we have identified various considerations that apparently have grown in importance as party has declined, but it is far from clear how such considerations might apply to the states. Consider North Dakota, a state whose recent pattern of party control is precisely the opposite of the national pattern. Democrats controlled the governor's mansion from 1960 to 1980, while the Republicans controlled the upper House for the same period.[8] Applying national-level arguments, we might ask, have North Dakota Republican legislators developed an incumbency advantage that enables them to withstand the Democratic gubernatorial tides? Or, does the North Dakota Republican party have a fractious gubernatorial nomination process that prevents them from uniting behind an executive candidate? Or, have North Dakota Republicans cunningly gerrymandered Democrats out of a fair share of legislative seats? Or, finally, do North Dakota Democratic executives benefit from a reputation as effective macro-economic managers while North Dakota Republican legislators benefit from a reputation as fair, compassionate protectors of the people? Each of the preceding arguments has been offered as an explanation of presidential-congressional splits, but it is doubtful that they shed much light on the North Dakota situation. Perhaps such arguments do have some relevance for state outcomes, but extending and/or modifying those arguments obviously will be necessary.

My belief is that when suitably generalized, some of the considerations offered as explanations of national divided government do apply to the states. Conversely, our understanding of national politics will benefit from the more general perspective encouraged by a consideration of the states' experiences. As a way of motivating those generalizations, I will review the patterns of election outcomes that have developed in the states. Several of these patterns suggest directions in which to proceed.

---

[8]The Republicans controlled the North Dakota House for sixteen of the twenty years; Democrats captured it in 1964 and 1976. Although the state was unified Republican for two years after the 1980 elections, the pattern of divided government otherwise has continued in the 1980s.

Trends and Patterns of Party Control in the States: Preliminaries

Upon learning that divided government in the states has increased, students of American politics predictably pose two questions. First: what about the South—to what extent does the decline in unified state government simply reflect the breakup of the once solid South? Figure 3-2 separates the Southern from the non-Southern states. Evidently, the South is not much to blame for the decline in unified state government. The breakup of the solid South at the state level does not begin until the 1960s, by which time the decline of unified government in the non-South is well underway. Variations in unified government after that time move together in both South and non-South, including the decline of unified government in the 1980s. Neither the earlier nor the later drops in unified government appear to be merely by-products of party realignment in the South.

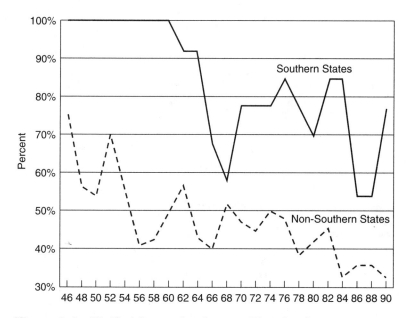

Figure 3-2   Unified States: South *versus* Non-South

Figures 3-1 and 3-2 also answer a second common question. Given the "reapportionment revolution" set in motion by the Supreme Court's apportionment decisions of 1962–65 ("one person, one vote"), might the decline in state unified government somehow reflect the wave of redistricting that took place in the mid- to late 1960s?[9] The data suggest otherwise. Much of the decline occurs prior to the court decisions, and there is a slight *resurgence* of unified government in the late 1960s consistent with Erikson's suggestion that reapportionment would lead to *less* divided government.[10] All in all, it is hard to argue that the reapportionment revolution had much, if anything, to do with the increase in divided government.

Thus, the broad outlines of divided government in the states suggest the most basic question for future research:

What factors have led to the decline of unified state government, especially the large drop in the first half of the post-war period?

Disaggregating the Trend: Parties and Institutions

With the exceptions of the unified Republican episode of 1952–54 and the Democratic-headed divided government episode of 1946–48, the past half century of national elections has yielded either unified Democratic government or divided government with Republican presidents. The states provide much more variation. More than half the states were unified Democratic after the 1974 elections; less than one-quarter were so after the 1968 elections. More than half the states were unified Republican after the 1952

---

[9]The seminal decision was *Baker v. Carr*, 369 U.S. 186 (1962).

[10]Although Erikson finds that reapportionment helped the Democratic party gain seats in state legislatures, the effect was not as large as many expected, possibly because rural Republicans lost seats to suburban Republicans. As for divided government, Hofferbert found that the degree of malapportionment between 1952 and 1962 was unrelated to divided control. Robert Erikson, "The Partisan Impact of State Legislative Reapportionment," *American Journal of Political Science* 15 (1971): 57–71; Richard I. Hofferbert, "The Relation Between Public Policy and Some Structural and Environmental Variables in the American States," *American Political Science Review* 60 (1966): 73–82.

Table 3-4 Trends in Divided State Government

1. %	Unified	=	.77 (30)	−	1.55 Election (7.93)	$R^2 = .75$
2. %	Republican	=	.38 (9.4)	−	1.60 Election (5.23)	$R^2 = .56$
3. %	Democratic	=	.39 (9.58)	−	.05 Election (.16)	$R^2 = .00$
4. %	Republican Governors	=	.45 (10.15)	−	.004 Election (1.16)	$R^2 = .02$
5. %	Republican Legislatures	=	.53 (10.4)	−	1.54 Election (3.96)	$R^2 = .41$
6. %	Democratic Legislatures	=	.47 (9.19)	+	1.54 Election (3.96)	$R^2 = .41$

Key: OLS regressions, *t* statistics in parentheses. Election: 1946 = 1, 1948 = 2, etc.

election; less than 5 percent were so after the 1974 elections (Figure 3-3). Divided governments of both kinds (Democratic executives, Republican executives) are present in some numbers.

While there has been quite a bit of fluctuation over time, Figure 3-3 and Table 3-4 (equations 2 and 3) indicate that the decline in unified state government largely reflects a fall in unified *Republican* state government: there is no trend in unified Democratic government, with comparable highs and lows before and after the 1968 trough, whereas the Republican figures show a sharp decline that parallels the national trend.[11]

Unified government is a concatenation of gubernatorial and legislative outcomes, so the logical next step is to examine those outcomes separately. Gubernatorial outcomes show no trend (Table 3-4, equation 4), although they are highly variable (Figure 3-4). The Democrats held less than 40 percent of the governorships following the 1952 and 1968 elections and more than 70 percent following the 1958 and 1974 elections. Republican outcomes are the mirror

[11]Following the 1990 elections, only South Dakota, New Hampshire, and Utah were under unified Republican control.

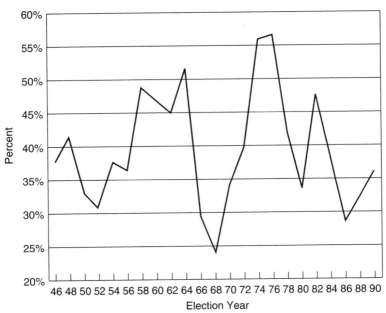

Figure 3-3 (A) Unified Democratic States

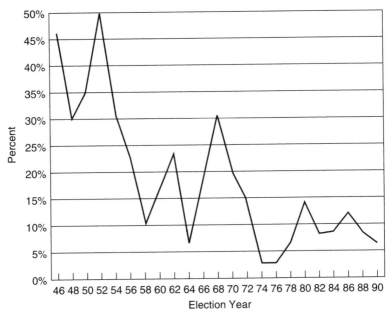

Figure 3-3 (B) Unified Republican States

34

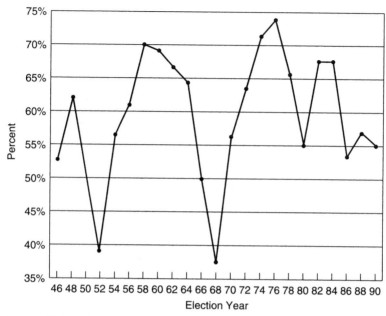

Figure 3-4 Democratic Governors

image, of course (except for a rare independent). Legislative outcomes reveal a different picture, however (Figure 3-5). There has been a clear increase in unified Democratic legislatures, or almost equivalently, a decline in unified Republican legislatures (Table 3-4, equations 5 and 6).[12] In the early post-war years Republicans controlled the legislatures of approximately half the states, but that figure dropped to less than one-quarter during the 1980s, with intermediate low points following the elections of 1958, 1964, and 1974–76. Following the 1990 elections the Republicans controlled only five state legislatures. Thus, the inability of Republicans to capture the U.S. House of Representatives since 1952 finds a reflection in the declining ability of Republicans to win legislative majorities in the American states.

[12]The two trends are almost mirror images because split legislatures are relatively rare (generally between 12 and 18 percent of the total) and show no trend.

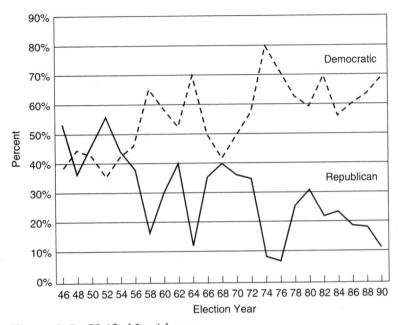

Figure 3-5   Unified Legislatures

As a consequence of the preceding developments, divided government with a Republican executive (the contemporary national pattern) and divided government with a Democratic executive (unknown on the national level since 1946) have become the second and third most common patterns of party control in the states (Figure 3-6). The obvious starting point in any explanation of these changing patterns of government control appears to be the precipitous decline in unified *Republican* state government, which in turn largely reflects a decline in Republican *legislatures*. Even without the decoupling of executive and legislative outcomes, the decline in Republican legislatures coupled with no trend in gubernatorial outcomes would have led to a decline in unified government, *ceteris paribus*. Thus we have a second question for future research:

What factors have contributed to the decline in Republican state legislative strength?

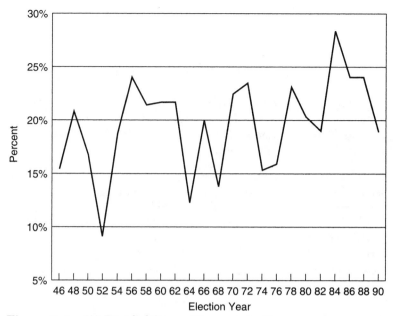

Figure 3-6 (A) Divided States: Democratic Governor

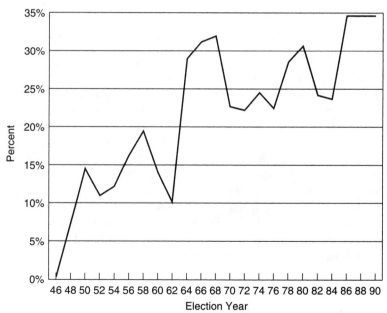

Figure 3-6 (B) Divided States: Republican Governor

37

Disaggregating the Trend: States

Measured by the percentage of years unified since 1946, the top ten unified government states include eight states of the old Confederacy plus Hawaii.[13] The second ten most unified states and the ten least unified states are as follows:

Second Ten Most Unified		Ten Least Unified	
South Dakota	81%	Michigan	14%
North Carolina	77	Nevada	19
Virginia	77	Montana	24
New Hampshire	76	Illinois	27
Maryland	73	Alaska	29
Oklahoma	73	Ohio	33
Tennessee	71	North Dakota	36
Minnesota	67	Maine	36
California	65	Delaware	36
Indiana	64	Utah	41

Aficionados of state politics may detect some subtle patterns, but for most of us these listings offer no obvious clues. South Dakota is unified, neighboring North Dakota is divided. Maryland is unified, neighboring Delaware is divided. Indiana is unified; neighboring Ohio is divided. Populous, heterogeneous California is unified, populous, heterogeneous Illinois is divided. The two groups seem indistinct.

Some clues emerge, however, upon differentiating between the Democratic- and Republican-headed divided states. With the decline in Republican state legislatures, the modal pattern of divided government has become like the national pattern: Republican executive, Democratic legislature. But there are also numerous examples of the opposite pattern—North Dakota is not unique. The ten most divided states of each type are as follows:

[13]Tabulations for Hawaii and Alaska are based on 1958 to 1990, for Minnesota from 1972 (when nonpartisan elections were eliminated) to 1990, and for other states from 1946 to 1990.

Democratic-Headed Divided		Republican-Headed Divided	
North Dakota	59%	Oregon	54%
Colorado	55	Delaware	46
Wyoming	50	Washington	46
Idaho	46	California	41
Kansas	46	Illinois	41
Michigan	46	Michigan	41
Nevada	46	Montana	36
New York	46	Nevada	36
Ohio	46	New Mexico	36
Maine	45	West Virginia	36

The Michigan and Nevada cases apparently reflect intensely competitive state party systems.[14] The remaining cases, however, support two observations. First, the Democratic-headed divided category includes more smaller states than the Republican-headed category—a total of ninety-two congressional districts in the former, as compared with 110 in the latter (as of the 1980s apportionment). Second, and more intriguing, in many cases gubernatorial outcomes in these states run counter to their popular national images, especially in the Democratic-headed divided government category. We think of the mountain states as rockribbed Republican, but they have elected Democratic governors almost half the time since World War II.[15] Ditto Maine. On the other side, few states are more Democratic than West Virginia, but her citizens show a certain

---

[14]Interestingly, an empirical problem in *explaining* split control by reference to party competition is that split control has been used to *measure* party competition. See, for example, the classic Ranney index and King's more recent discussion. Austin Ranney, "Parties in State Politics," in Herbert Jacob and Kenneth Vines, eds., *Politics in the American States: A Comparative Analysis* (Boston: Little, Brown, 1965), chap. 3; James King, "Interparty Competition in the American States: An Examination of Index Components," *Western Political Quarterly* 42 (1989): 83–92.

[15]In addition to the two, three, and four spots held by Colorado, Wyoming, and Idaho, two other mountain states, Montana and Utah, tie for twelfth on the Democratic-headed divided government list with 41 percent.

Table 3-5   Correlations between State Partisanship[a]
            and Patterns of Government

% Years	
Unified Democratic	+.79
Divided: Democratic governor	–.62
Divided: Republican governor	+.48
Unified Republican	–.64

[a]Partisanship runs from strongly Republican (–) to strongly
Democratic (+).

fondness for Republican governors.[16] In fact, outside the South
there is an interesting correlation between a state's partisanship and
patterns of party control. The more partisan the state, the more
years of unified government under the advantaged party *and* the
more years of divided government under an executive of the disad-
vantaged party (Table 3-5).[17] Again, this resembles the national pattern, where a Democratic advantage in partisanship has long
coexisted with Republican presidential majorities. Thus, we pose a
third question for future research:

Relative to the partisan composition of their states, why do minority party
executive candidates seem to do better than expected?

Summary

This quick survey of patterns of government in the American states
reveals three interesting findings, *each of which resembles a characteris-*

[16]So do the citizens of Massachusetts and Rhode Island, which tie for eleventh on the
Republican-headed divided government list with 32 percent.

[17]State partisanship is based on pooled data (1976–82) from CBS/*NYT* exit polls.
Thirty-eight states show an excess of Democrats over Republicans and ten the
opposite (no data are available for Hawaii and Alaska). The data are described in
Robert S. Erikson, John P. McIver, and Gerald C. Wright, Jr., "State Political Culture
and Public Opinion," *American Political Science Review* 81 (1987): 797–813. I am
grateful to Gerald Wright for providing these data.

tic of the recent national experience. (1) We noted earlier the historical uniqueness of the 1956 national elections, in which ticket-splitting was sufficiently widespread that for the first time in our history a president victorious in a two-way race failed to carry the House. Apparently, much the same thing happened in state elections at about the same time, as unified state government plunged almost 25 percent between the 1952 and 1956 elections. In addition, the correlation between divided government at the two levels holds at the cross-sectional as well as the aggregate level; there is a clear correlation between divided government in a state and presidential–House splits in the same state. In the 1988 elections, for example, 23 percent of the congressional districts in unified states split their presidential and House majorities, whereas twice as large a proportion—45 percent—were split in divided states. (2) Much of the decline in unified government in the states reflects the disappearance of Republican legislative majorities, just as the disappearance of Republican majorities in the House of Representatives is a large part of the explanation of the decline in unified national government. (3) In state elections divided government seems to arise from voters' leaning against state partisanship when choosing executives. The same pattern is evident on the national level, as voters have chosen Republican executives in seven of the past ten elections, while never favoring the Republicans over the Democrats when reporting their party identification.[18]

Afterthought: The Puzzle of U.S. Senate Elections

United States senators are chosen in statewide elections to serve in the national Congress. As such, one might expect their elections to have something in common with other statewide elections, such as those for governor. Post-war Senate elections show an interesting development, namely, a pronounced increase in the tendency of

---

[18]Based on data from the American National Election Studies. By 1988 the Republicans had achieved virtual parity with the Democrats, when they trailed by only 1 percent, 47–46 (classifying independent leaners as partisans).

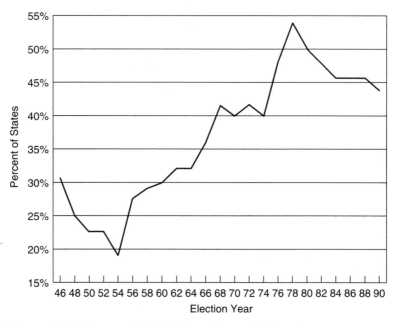

Figure 3-7   States with Split-Party Senate Delegations

states to divide their Senate representation between the two parties
(Figure 3-7). As Shapiro, Brady, Brody, and Ferejohn observe:

> In the 1918–1958 period, only three congresses had mixed party repre-
> sentation in more than 30 percent of the state delegations; since 1960
> no Congress has had less than 30 percent such delegations. Since 1966
> the percentage of mixed-party delegations has not fallen below 40 per-
> cent; in 1978 the percentage rose to 54 percent.[19]

It is not clear what to make of this development. On the one
hand, the concept of divided government refers to control of different
governmental institutions—upper chamber, lower chamber, the executive—by different parties, while divided Senate delegations occur

---

[19]Catherine R. Shapiro, David W Brady, Richard A. Brody, and John A. Ferejohn,
"Linking Constituency Opinion and Senate Voting Scores: A Hybrid Model,"
Legislative Studies Quarterly 15 (1990): 599–621.

within one institution. On the other hand, it is reasonable to suspect that there is some relation between the increase in divided government in the states and the increase in divided Senate delegations.

If the two developments are to any significant degree the result of a common impulse, the implications for some explanations of divided government obviously are negative. Strategic drawing of district lines can have nothing whatsoever to do with split Senate delegations, since state boundaries are inviolate. Similarly, differences in nominating processes and contrasting perceptions of the comparative strengths of executive and legislative institutions can have nothing to do with split delegations, since both senators of a state are nominated in the same manner and both are legislators. Incumbency would seem to have little relevance since more often than not both senators are incumbents. What then? We return to this puzzle later.

...

So, in the last half of the twentieth century a critical minority of voters have decided to split their tickets between president and representative, and between governor and state legislator, and to alternate between voting for Democratic and Republican senators. Why has all of this seemingly schizophrenic electoral behavior developed? Enough of questions. It is time to consider answers.

CHAPTER 4

EXPLANATIONS I:

UNINTENDED CONSEQUENCES

The preceding chapters show that divided government is not a simple phenomenon. It is a condition that occurs on the state as well as the national level, it is correlated across the two levels, and it may be related as well to such things as the increasing party splits in Senate delegations. All of this suggests, in turn, that there is no single explanation for divided government: its multifacets may reflect multiple causes. Thus far, we have uncovered more facets than causes. We have seen that gerrymandering does not explain the national condition, and it is unlikely that it has much to do with the varied state conditions. We have seen that incumbency is not a complete explanation for the national condition, and it has not been proposed as a major explanation for state divided government.[1] What then?

Party decline is a traditional favorite. Supposedly, as party loyalties weaken, voters increasingly split their tickets, picking and choosing among the parties' nominees according to their positions, personalities, TV commercials, or whatever. Party decline is relevant, of course: where parties rigorously structure the electorate, there is no split-ticket voting, and, thus, much of the basis of divided government disappears.[2] But party decline is a precondition rather

---

[1]Malcolm Jewell and David Breaux provide an extensive analysis of the advantage of incumbency in state legislative elections, though they do not address the question of divided government. "The Effect of Incumbency on State Legislative Elections," *Legislative Studies Quarterly* 13 (1988): 495–514.

[2]Not all, though. Where elections are independent *and* staggered in time, divided government still can occur. Recall the prevalence of divided government after midterm elections in the nineteenth century.

than an explanation. Once the bonds between the electorate and the parties weaken, other factors can affect voting behavior. Are such other factors random or systematic? If there were nothing beyond the more or less random distribution of candidate personalities and campaign ads, outcomes would be similarly random. Divided governments would occur, but without the trends, asymmetries, and correlations that we have found. The latter suggest that something else is at work. In thinking about the possible somethings, I have found it useful to classify possibilities into two general categories: (1) those factors that might have affected the behavior of politicians and (2) those factors that might have affected the behavior of voters. Strictly speaking, such a separation is impossible—voters and politicians are partners in the electoral dance—but the categorization is a rough way of focusing on which partner might have taken the lead as they danced into the second half of the twentieth century. Let us begin by considering the decline of Republican legislative strength.

Candidates, Parties, and Professional Legislatures

Party prospects in state legislative races clearly rise and fall with presidential outcomes. In both state and nation, Republican low points were reached in the Democratic landslides of 1958, 1964, and 1974, while high points were reached in 1952, 1968, and 1980 (Figure 3–5). A complete analysis should parse out the state-level variation that reflects national forces.[3] Over and above the impact of national elections, however, Republican legislatures clearly had been in decline in the post-war period until 1994; at the state legislative level the Reagan tidal wave of 1980 did not match the narrow Nixon victory of 1968, and Reagan's "personal" victory in 1984 had nowhere near the impact of Nixon's in 1972. And then there was the hopeless condition of Republicans in the U.S. House since 1954.

[3]For analyses of national effects in state elections, see John Chubb, "Institutions, the Economy, and the Dynamics of State Elections," *American Political Science Review* 82 (1988): 133–54; James Piereson, "Presidential Popularity and Midterm Voting at Different Electoral Levels," *American Journal of Political Science* 19 (1975): 683–94; and Dennis Simon, "Presidents, Governors, and Electoral Accountability," *Journal of Politics* 51 (1989): 286–304.

In reflecting on the former predicament of the Republican minority in the House of Representatives, Jacobson properly dismisses a number of the more commonly offered excuses.[4] Gerrymandering is not the problem, nor is the Democrats' vaunted edge in PAC financing—since 1972 Republican incumbents have outspent Democrats in every election except 1984; Republican challengers have outspent Democrats in every election except 1974, 1986, and 1988; and Republican nominees in open seats have outspent Democrats from 1980 to the present. Jacobson argues that PAC contributions to Democrats are a symptom, not a cause: as measured by previous political experience, Republican candidates on average simply are a weak lot, not worth the investment of shrewd campaign contributors.

Why would one party systematically field poorer candidates than the other? As noted earlier, Ehrenhalt suggests that Republican ideology is part of the problem. If the potential candidate pool of one party consists of people who believe in using public authority, while the potential candidate pool of the other consists of people skeptical of government action, the former will be more likely to run, and once successful, to use government programs to enhance their reelection prospects. Jacobson appears to concur.[5] The argument is attractive, but Gelman and King find no difference in the incumbency advantage of Democrats and Republicans, suggesting that the latter are equally good at using government once they win office.[6] As for the lack of motivation to enter politics in the first place, Zupan poses a reasonable question: why should potential conservative representatives not anticipate as much pleasure from tearing down government as liberals anticipate from expanding it?[7]

Could there be other reasons that a greater number of capable and attractive Democrats run for legislative office than capable and attractive Republicans? Perhaps we focus too much on the ideological benefits and costs of holding office and too little on other kinds

---

[4]Gary Jacobson, *The Electoral Origins of Divided Government* (Boulder, CO: Westview Press, 1990), chap. 5.

[5]Jacobson, *Electoral Origins*, 120–22.

[6]Andrew Gelman and Gary King, "Estimating Incumbency Advantage Without Bias," *American Journal of Political Science* 34 (1990): 1158.

[7]Mark Zupan, "An Economic Explanation for the Existence and Nature of Political Ticket Splitting," *Journal of Law and Economics* 34(1991): 343–369.

of benefits and costs. One possibility that merits investigation is that Republican legislatures have declined as an accidental by-product or unintended consequence of "progressive" reforms that altered the non-policy benefits and costs of holding legislative office. To illustrate, consider two polar cases.

Case 1. Wyoming: 1950 *versus* 1990

Wyoming is indisputably a glorious state, but service in its legislature has never been one of its more notable attractions. In the early post-war years, representatives were paid $12 a day and received a $6 per diem during the session. This did not amount to much since the legislature met every other year and was limited to a 40-day session. No major perks went along with office. Turnover was about 50 percent per election.[8]

Of course, since 1950 the pay and responsibilities of Wyoming legislators have increased. Today they receive $75 per day with a $60 per diem. The legislature may now meet for 20 days during the even years as well as 40 during the odd years. But relative to other states, the Wyoming legislature continues to occupy a position near the amateur end of the amateur–professional continuum. Perks are few and turnover remains relatively high—about 33 percent per election.[9] Perhaps coincidentally, perhaps not, in the post-war period Wyoming has never elected a Democratic Senate, and only twice (1958, 1964), a Democratic House.[10]

Case 2. California: 1950 *versus* 1990

The contemporary California legislature epitomizes the professional pole of the amateur–professional dimension, although recent passage of a terms limitation initiative may alter this state of affairs. Its members currently receive $40,816 salaries, $88 per diems, state-leased

[8]Kwang S. Shin and John S. Jackson III, "Membership Turnover in U.S. State Legislatures: 1931–1976," *Legislative Studies Quarterly* 4 (1979): Table 1.
[9]Richard G. Niemi and Laura R. Winsky, "Membership Turnover in U.S. State Legislatures: Trends and Effects of Redistricting," *Legislative Studies Quarterly* 12 (1987): Table 1.
[10]The two parties tied in the Senate in 1974 and in the House in 1948.

automobiles, and retirement benefits. Like Congress, the California legislature meets more or less year-round, and the members have full-time personal staffs. Turnover is less than 20 percent per election.[11]

Even in the early post-war years, California legislators were comparatively well supported, with a $3,600 annual salary and $12 per diem. Session limits were relatively generous—120 days per year, with an additional 30-day budget session permitted in even years. Turnover rates were about half those of Wyoming.[12] Perhaps coincidentally, perhaps not, the Democrats had taken control of the California legislature by 1958 (for the first time since 1938). Since then they have never lost the Senate (a tie in 1968) and lost the House only in 1968.

These examples differ across many important dimensions. Nevertheless, they suggest a hypothesis that can be examined in a systematic fashion: other things being equal, amateur legislatures favor Republicans while more professionalized legislatures favor Democrats.

Candidates who seek to serve in amateur legislatures probably differ in systematic ways from those who seek to serve in professional legislatures. Because service is part-time and poorly remunerated, candidates must have independent sources of income and/or the freedom to take time away from primary occupations without undue financial or career costs. Conversely, the candidacies of individuals with little discretionary income and jobs that demand their continual presence will be discouraged—how many people who work for hourly wages are in a position to take a month or two off each year? Thus, amateur political settings advantage the independently wealthy (and those with wealthy families), professionals with private practices, independent business people, and others with similar financial and career flexibility.[13] As Nike spokesman, Mr. Robinson, might say, "How do you spell *Republicans*, boys and girls?"

---

[11]Niemi and Winsky, Table 1.

[12]Shin and Jackson, Table 1.

[13]This is, of course, a common finding in the older literature, when most state legislatures were amateur. See Charles Hyneman, "Tenure and Turnover of Legislative Personnel," *Annals of the American Academy of Political and Social Science* 190 (1938): 21–31. The definitive modern texts agree that lawyers and businessmen have long dominated the state legislative scene. Malcolm E. Jewell and Samuel C. Patterson, *The Legislative Process in the United States* (New York: Random House, 1986), 50; William J. Keefe and Morris S. Ogul, *The American Legislative Process* (Englewood Cliffs, NJ: Prentice-Hall, 1985), 111–13.

Professional legislatures generate quite different incentives. The average compensation of legislators in California, New York, and a number of other states exceeds median *household* income (about $38,000), and generous expense allowances, tax deductions, and leadership bonuses add significantly to their salaries.[14] For many capable individuals in Democratic population groups, service in such a legislature would be an alternative career more attractive than others open to them.[15] Conversely, as legislative service becomes a full-time pursuit, it becomes less attractive to capable people in Republican population groups unable or unwilling to abandon more lucrative careers in the private sector even for comparatively well-compensated—but full-time—legislative positions. Ehrenhalt makes the additional point that even *seeking* election to many offices has become more than a full-time job. Thus, even those who would be willing to serve might not be willing to do what is required to win.[16]

Thus, as legislatures professionalize—as they become full-time institutions with respectable salaries and perks, professional staffs, and responsibility for overseeing billion-dollar state expenditures, there should be an erosion of the recruitment advantage Republicans enjoy in more amateurish situations. The Democratic candidate pool should grow in both quantity and quality. This argument is analogous to that advanced by European parties of the left when they advocated salaries for parliamentarians, and in fact goes back at least to Aristotle.[17] Consider the argument against legislative salaries made by John Stuart Mill, a major theorist of representation:

[14]For a discussion of the attractions of service in the contemporary New York state legislature, see Linda L. Fowler and Robert D. McClure, *Political Ambition* (New Haven, CT: Yale University Press, 1989).

[15]According to Keefe and Ogul, "the fastest growing occupational group among state legislators is that of educators." *American Legislative Process,* 112. Predominantly public sector employees, educators are disproportionately Democratic.

[16]Ehrenhalt, *The United States of Ambition,* passim.

[17]Aristotle comments that "Pericles was also the first to introduce payment for service on the law courts.... Some people blame him on this account and say that the law courts deteriorated, since after that it was always the common men rather than the better men who were eager to participate in drawing the lot for duty in the law courts." Kurt von Fritz, *Aristotle's Constitution of Athens and Related Texts* (New York: Hafner, 1964), 97–98. I am indebted to Steven Macedo for this reference.

No remuneration which anyone would think of attaching to the post would attract to it those who were seriously engaged in other lucrative professions with a prospect of succeeding in them. The business of a member of Parliament would therefore become an occupation in itself; carried on, like other professions, with a view chiefly to its pecuniary returns, and under the demoralizing influences of an occupation essentially precarious. It would become an object of desire to adventurers of a low class; and 658 in possession, with ten or twenty times as many in expectancy, would be incessantly bidding to attract or retain the suffrages of the electors, by promising all things, honest or dishonest, possible or impossible, and rivaling each other in pandering to the meanest feelings and most ignorant prejudices of the vulgarest part of the crowd.[18]

Mill's elitist bias is not the issue here. What is of interest is his contention that legislative salaries would change the composition of Parliament from a body composed of successful people from lucrative professions to one composed of "adventurers of a low class." Given the social bases of political parties, this implies that legislative salaries advantage parties of the left relative to those of the right, or meaning no insult, Democrats relative to Republicans.

The professionalization of legislatures generally is cloaked in public interest rationales: the world grows increasingly complicated, so legislatures must increase their expertise; the executive grows increasingly powerful, so representative assemblies must keep pace. No doubt there is much validity in such arguments. But there is similarly no doubt that much of the increased staff and other resources that professional legislators control is put to electoral uses. In a study of thirteen state legislatures over the period 1968–86, King has shown that the advantage of incumbency is directly related to the size of the legislative operating budget.[19] Weber, Tucker, and Brace show that "institutionalization" (i.e., professionalism) is associated with higher victory margins and fewer contested seats in fourteen state lower houses over a thirty-six-year period.[20] Holbrook and

---

[18]H. B. Acton, ed., *John Stuart Mill, Utilitarianism, On Liberty, and Considerations on Representative Government* (London: J. M. Dent & Sons, 1972), 311.

[19]Gary King, "Constituency Service and Incumbency Advantage," *British Journal of Political Science* 21 (1991): 119–28.

[20]Ronald Weber, Harvey Tucker, and Paul Brace, "Vanishing Marginals in State Legislative Elections," *Legislative Studies Quarterly* 16 (1991): 29–47.

Tidmarch show that "sophomore surges" (the vote gain between an incumbent's initial election and first reelection) are significantly larger in legislatures with larger personal staffs.[21] In sum, professional legislators are advantaged in the electoral arena.

As this discussion intimates, the House incumbency explanation of national divided government is related to the more general professionalism argument. Congress is undoubtedly the most professional of the world's legislatures.[22] It has an elaborate committee structure and a large supporting bureaucracy, and its members are quite well supported and compensated.[23] As Congress transformed itself from an amateur to a professional institution, turnover dropped and tenure rose—until the late nineteenth-century Congress looked much like Wyoming.[24] But it is not incumbency *per se* that advantages Democrats; earlier we examined that argument and found it wanting. Professionalization gives advantages to incumbents of *both* parties once they are incumbents, but professionalization encourages Democrats, more than Republicans, to try to become incumbents in the first place.

An important feature of this explanation for declining Republican legislative strength is its self-reinforcing quality. First, as qualified Republicans decline to seek state legislative office, the Republican party increasingly becomes a minority party, which diminishes its influence over policy and thereby further diminishes its attraction to potential candidates. Moreover, as the pool of Republican state legislators grows smaller, the pool of candidates for the U.S. House declines correspondingly.[25] As minority status in the House increas-

---

[21]Thomas Holbrook and Charles Tidmarch, "Sophomore Surge in State Legislative Elections," *Legislative Studies Quarterly* 16 (1991): 49–63.

[22]Nelson W. Polsby, "Legislatures," in Fred I. Greenstein and Nelson W. Polsby, eds., *Handbook of Political Science*, Vol. 5 (Reading, MA: Addison-Wesley, 1975), passim.

[23]Norman J. Ornstein, Thomas E. Mann, and Michael Malbin, eds., *Vital Statistics on Congress: 1989–1990* (Washington, DC: Congressional Quarterly Inc., 1990), chaps. 4–5.

[24]Nelson W. Polsby, "The Institutionalization of the U.S. House of Representatives," *American Political Science Review* 62 (1968): 144–68. H. Douglas Price, "Congress and the Evolution of Legislative 'Professionalism,'" in Norman Ornstein, ed., *Congress in Change* (New York: Praeger, 1975), 2–23.

[25]Canon reports that in recent years the proportion of members of Congress coming from state legislatures has grown. Thus, recruitment to Congress is based on an increasingly Democratic candidate pool. David T. Canon, *Actors, Athletes, and Astronauts* (Chicago: University of Chicago Press, 1990), 53–56.

ingly appeared to be a permanent condition, the attractiveness of House service to potential Republican candidates dwindled. Weakness begets weakness. However, 1994 changed things dramatically.

Second, as discussed above, professionalization makes at least some contribution to the increased advantage of incumbency in the U.S. House: members intent on reelection and in possession of electorally valuable resources have the motive and opportunity to build individual coalitions based on personal contact and district service. These "personal" constituencies partially insulate them from the winds of electoral change that blow across the presidential landscape.[26] In general, professionalized legislatures are more electorally insulated than less professionalized ones.[27] Thus, professionalism not only affects the relative attraction of legislative careers for the two parties, but also would further serve to insulate those candidates who do seek and win office. If the argument is correct, this means Democrats. That is, Democratic candidates will find the job more attractive, and once they have it they will be likely to retain it. They will do no better in this respect than Republicans, consistent with Gelman and King's finding, but their initial selection advantage will be preserved in future elections.

This brings us in a very roundabout way to a subject that is currently attracting much attention: the terms limitation movement. Consistent with the charges of some partisan commentators, the argument about legislative professionalization developed here has important implications for proposals to limit legislative terms.

---

[26]Bruce Cain, John Ferejohn, and Morris Fiorina, *The Personal Vote* (Cambridge, Mass.: Harvard University Press, 1987); Steven Ansolabehere, David Brady, and Morris Fiorina, "The Marginals Never Vanished?" *British Journal of Political Science* 22 (1992): 121–38.

[27]This argument was anticipated by Asher in the late 1970s when he cautioned that reforms intended to professionalize state legislatures would tend to insulate incumbents in office. It is unfortunate that his argument did not receive more attention. Herbert B. Asher, "The Unintended Consequences of Legislative Professionalism," presented at the 1978 Annual Meeting of the American Political Science Association, September, New York.

The Terms Limitation Movement

In the 1990 elections, voters in California and Colorado approved ballot initiatives that would limit the length of service of their state legislators.[28] Earlier Oklahoma had done the same. The terms limitation movement has gained strength in recent years, and the 1992 elections saw further attempts to cap the length of legislative service in the states. This particular reform thrust reflects a number of concerns. First, there is a widespread impression that incumbent legislators are invulnerable; the 96–98 percent reelection rates of U.S. representatives in the previous four elections certainly have contributed to that impression. (1994 was a departure from that trend.) Second, there is an impression that incumbent success is somehow unfair or illegitimate; the large "war chests" of PAC funds amassed by incumbents certainly have contributed to that impression, Third, there is a widespread feeling that legislatures are not performing well, although this belief is a quasi-permanent feature of American public opinion, perhaps reinforced by the recent economic hard times in many areas.[29]

Unlike the public, few academic analysts support terms limitations. My use of the noun *impressions* in the preceding paragraph was quite deliberate. However well meaning, the terms limitation movement is premised on a series of inaccurate impressions. Consequently, it misdiagnoses the situation. Moreover, like most reforms, this one is likely to have consequences other than those its proponents expressly seek. It is time to quit calling them "unanticipated consequences" when bemoaning them after the fact and think a bit about anticipating them before the fact.

---

[28]California limited service in the Assembly to three two-year terms and in the Senate to two four-year terms. Colorado imposed an eight-consecutive-year limit on both houses. The Colorado initiative also capped congressional terms at twelve years, but the power of state electorates to cap the terms of federal office-holders is dubious. The matter is now in the courts.

[29]According to a CBS News/*New York Times* survey taken a month before the 1990 elections (11 October 1990 press release), approval of the way Congress was handling its job stood at 27 percent, and 71 percent of the respondents said that more members were mainly interested in serving the special interests than the general interest.

Incumbents in many states and in Congress are very tough to beat, but they are not invulnerable. Members of the House do not win 95 percent of the time because they are unbeatable; rather, they win 95 percent of the time because they work so very hard at it. Huge war chests surely are a means to victory, but they also signify how worried members are even with no serious challenge in sight. Those who have studied them most closely agree that members of Congress "run scared."[30] To the observer a 95 percent success rate means representatives have nothing to worry about; but not being statisticians, and with their careers on the line, members focus on the exceptions—those few unfortunates who lose—not the rule. Because the exceptions are so unpredictable, members live in a condition of what Robert Weissberg calls "random terror." Rather than being unresponsive, representatives behave in an opposite way: members are regularly accused of crossing the line from responsiveness to pandering. Why would politicians who are invulnerable pander to anyone?

If 95 percent reelection rates do not necessarily indicate invulnerable, unresponsive *members*, neither do they necessarily indicate an ossified, unresponsive *institution*. If turnover were concentrated in the *same* 5 percent election after election, there would be cause for worry. But as Robert Erikson pointed out long ago, a surprisingly large proportion of members come to Congress by defeating the previous incumbent in a primary or general election (more than one-third), and leave via their own primary or general election defeat (more than one-third).[31] In the late 1980s the proportion had fallen somewhat, but many members have electoral close shaves that remind them and their colleagues of their potential vulnerability.[32] A much larger proportion of the membership of the House has some

---

[30]Richard F. Fenno, Jr., *Home Style* (Boston: Little, Brown, 1978), 10–18; Gary Jacobson, "Running Scared: Elections and Congressional Politics in the 1980s," in Mathew McCubbins and Terry Sullivan, eds., *Congress: Structure and Policy* (Cambridge, England: Cambridge University Press, 1987), 39–81.

[31]Robert S. Erikson, "Is There Such a Thing as a Safe Seat?" *Polity* 8 (1976): 623–32.

[32]For example, 38 percent of the representatives in the 102nd Congress had won at least one election *other than their initial one* with less than 60 percent of the vote. Joseph Gentile, "The Competitiveness of Elections in the U.S. House of Representatives," unpublished paper, Harvard University, 1991.

personal acquaintance with electoral vulnerability than overall reelection rates would suggest. All things considered—defeats, deaths, and resignations—few specialists in the field lose sleep over the purported petrification of Congress: more than one-half of the current membership has been elected since 1980, and average length of service is only a bit over five terms.

What about the third impression: that our national and state legislatures are failing in their jobs? Well, that is another matter. As a citizen of Massachusetts and the United States, I admit to regular feelings of unease as I watch our legislatures. But as political scientists pointed out long ago, a considerable portion of Congress's poor performance stems directly from the members' conscientious efforts to serve their constituents.[33] Members do not hesitate to fight for failing savings and loans, billion dollar weapons boondoggles, and ineffective programs of all types, so long as the waste (and worse) such programs entail accrues to the benefit of their local economies. Of course, the inevitable result of the representatives of 435 individual districts and fifty states seeking to benefit their own is that the nation suffers. If every district tries to benefit at the expense of others, then on balance none will benefit. If no district will bear any costs for the national good, then the national good will not be achieved. Ironically, if our legisla*tors* were less vulnerable and less responsive, they might be more willing to make tough, but nationally beneficial decisions, and we would probably rate our legisla*tures* more highly.

If the only problem with the terms limitation movement were that it misread the situation, professional legislators would be the only ones with cause for worry. But the likely consequences of terms limitation should give pause to ordinary citizens as well. Reform movements typically make a naive assumption that if power can be taken from the special interests who are the objects of the reforms,

---

[33]The seminal paper is Richard F. Fenno, Jr., "If, as Ralph Nader Says, Congress Is 'the Broken Branch,' How Come We Love Our Congressmen So Much?" in N. J. Ornstein, ed., *Congress in Change*, 277–87. See also Glenn R. Parker and Roger Davidson, "Why Do Americans Love Their Congressman So Much More than Their Congress?" *Legislative Studies Quarterly* 4 (1979): 53–62; Cain, Ferejohn, and Fiorina, *The Personal Vote*, chap. 8.

then it will devolve to ordinary citizens. Unfortunately, reality is such that when one special interest loses power, a different one generally gains. Terms limitation will probably have this effect.

In the first place, within the legislature power would probably flow to the staff. The members would have less time to accrue technical expertise and that intangible "institutional memory" that is vital in any organization. Fine, you say. Let's do away with the permanent staff. Let legislators manage with a few secretaries to answer mail and the phones. Well, aside from impairing the ability of members to service their constituencies, the likely result would be that power would shift to the executive branch, where the permanent bureaucracy would become the principal source of expertise and experience. Assuming that the bureaucracy cannot be eliminated, the only way for an amateur legislature to avoid reliance on the executive would be to rely more heavily on interest groups than it presently does. These groups undoubtedly would be happy to provide the expertise legislators need. Of course, the most disenchanted among us might claim that we *already* are governed by legislative staff, bureaucrats, and interest groups, but term limitations almost certainly would make this complaint less of an exaggeration than it is.

In my view the most serious negative consequence of terms limitations would be its effect on legislator incentives. Consider members of Congress. Currently, they have the option of planning to spend a career in the Congress. Not all will: some will opt to try for higher office, some will quit, and a few will be defeated. Those who leave with useful years remaining usually have the option of taking executive appointments or six-figure jobs as Washington lobbyists. If terms were limited, what would happen? As soon as members took office they would begin thinking about where their income would be coming from six to twelve years hence. They would *immediately* begin planning the next move—to a higher office (these are scarce), to an appointive position (high-level ones are also scarce), or to a lucrative position in the private sector (most likely). *Some* do that now, as mentioned above, but *everyone* would be looking ahead if there were a term limitation. Such a reform almost certainly would enhance the power of interest groups inasmuch as all legislators would be thinking of themselves as potential job applicants. The performance of contemporary legislatures is admittedly disheartening on occasion; terms limitations would not make matters better.

From the standpoint of this chapter, however, there is yet another consequence of terms limitation, one whose evaluation depends on the political predispositions of the reader. What proponents of terms limitation refer to as "citizen legislatures" are what political scientists call "amateur legislatures." Recall the Wyoming legislature circa 1950. Severely constrained in terms of how long it could sit, lacking staff, and paid but a pittance, one-half the Wyoming legislators departed every two years. This is the vision held by proponents of terms limitations. Whether they consciously realize it or not, if the professionalism argument advanced earlier is correct, an additional element of their vision of citizen legislatures is that these legislatures are Republican.[34]

If Republican legislative strength has declined as state legislatures have professionalized, then the same logic operating in reverse should lead to a revival of Republican prospects if legislatures are statutorily or constitutionally "de-professionalized." If the California vote withstands court challenge, legislative pensions will be eliminated, salaries cut, and terms limited to six years. What kinds of people will seek the office then? Will school teachers and other public employees give up job security and seniority to serve six years in the legislature? Hardly. On the other hand, large law firms and corporations may well detail junior partners and vice presidents to serve as legislators. Rather than lobby legislators, interest groups can simply pay employees to serve. In all likelihood the changes in California will lower the proportion of Democrats eager to serve and raise the proportion of Republicans.

There is another likely effect of terms limitation whose partisan consequences are harder to gauge. The leaders of single-issue groups will be able to combine part-time legislative service with full-time leadership of their groups. Thus, we might see an increase in the direct representation of "issue activists" on both ends of the political spectrum: pro-life *and* pro-choice, and so forth.

All in all, whatever the consequences of terms limitation, they are unlikely to be politically neutral. Reversing the movement toward professional legislatures should work to the advantage of

[34]Republicans have embraced the terms limitation movement more enthusiastically than Democrats, but it does seem to cut across party lines. It is worth noting that the Colorado legislature is heavily Republican while the California legislature is heavily Democratic.

Republican candidacies. Republican readers may understandably regard that as sufficiently important to bear the other likely costs of terms limitation. Democratic readers should be forewarned.

Summary

A large element in the increased incidence of divided government—both nationally and in the states—is the decline in Republican legislative strength. The fortunes of Republican gubernatorial candidates have waxed and waned but show no overall trend, and the fortunes of Republican presidential candidates show a great deal of waxing and precious little waning. If Republican legislative candidates had matched the performance of executive candidates, there would be less divided government and more unified Republican government in both states and nation.

In Chapter 2 we saw that House incumbency was not a sufficient explanation for divided national government, but in this chapter I have argued that a more general version of that argument—the long-term trend toward professionalized legislatures—may play a role in the decline of Republican legislative strength. It is not so much that Republicans do worse once they achieve legislative office; rather, consistent with Jacobson's findings, potential Republican candidates are less likely to seek the office in the first place. Full-time legislative careers have higher opportunity costs for Republicans, who have more attractive alternatives in business and the professions. Conversely, full-time careers are more attractive to Democrats who have lower opportunity costs given their ordinary career alternatives. Moreover, once Republicans fall to minority status, their chances of achieving programmatic or ideological goals decline, further diminishing the attractiveness of legislative candidacies.

A direct implication of this argument is that, however well-intended, some "good government" reforms have partisan consequences. The successful effort to professionalize state legislatures probably worked against Republicans. Successful efforts to reverse that trend, such as terms limitation, are likely to work against Democrats.

Explanations II: Do Voters Choose Divided Government?

The preceding chapter addressed one important element in the increased incidence of divided government in the United States: poor Republican showings in legislative races. According to the principal hypothesis offered—increased legislative professionalism—this element of divided government is partly an accident, a by-product of a series of institutional changes that reflect independent or unrelated motives. (I do not think it plausible to argue that the advocates of legislative professionalism had a hidden agenda of doing in the Republican party.) It would not be the first time nor will it be the last time that governmental reform had unanticipated consequences.

But there is another major element of divided government that we have not yet addressed. Chapter 3 showed that executive and legislative outcomes have become increasingly disconnected. Moreover, states that lean Democratic in their partisanship and presidential voting behavior frequently elect Republican governors, mimicking the national pattern of divided control. The remaining "Republican" states show an even more noteworthy tendency to elect Democratic governors—recall the unusual electoral history of the mountain states. Executive elections seem somewhat at odds with what popular images and state legislative elections would lead one to expect.

Of course, the same is true of the nation as a whole. Consider Figure 5-1, which charts the partisanship of the national electorate in each presidential campaign since 1952.[1] At the same time that the

---

[1]The data are from the biennial American National Election Studies (ANES). Strong and weak identifiers are classified as partisans, though the outlines of the figure and its implications would not change if leaning independents were included as partisans.

national electorate was choosing Republican presidents—seven of the ten elections—it regularly gave the Democrats a plurality of its party loyalties. There are any number of explanations for why Democrats lose the presidency. Some Democratic politicos claim that the Republicans field candidates with superior personalities (swallowing hard when Richard Nixon and George Bush are mentioned). Republicans claim that on important issues—race, taxes, values, and defense—a leftward-lurching Democratic party abandoned the great middle ground. But such explanations do not explain why partisan loyalties have been so slow to change along with presidential votes.

From the standpoint of this essay, a more important difficulty is that the national pattern appears to be only a special case of a general pattern, whereupon electorates, whether Republican or Democratic, seem much more willing to vote counter to their partisan inclinations when choosing executives than when choosing legislators. As yet we have no explanation for this larger pattern. Can we

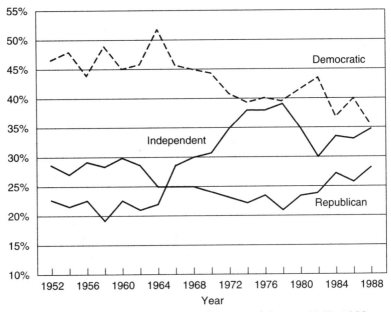

Figure 5-1   Party Identification in the United States: 1952–1988

seriously argue that North Dakota Democratic gubernatorial candidates invariably have more attractive personalities than their Republican opponents, and that the opposite is true in Oregon? Can we argue that Democratic gubernatorial candidates win in Colorado because the Republican party has lurched rightward, while the opposite is true in the state of Washington? Explanations tailored for specific cases fail to generalize convincingly to the larger universe of cases. There appears to be some method to the electorate's decisions, but what is it?

The Possibility of Artifact

Before considering substantive explanations for the frequency of minority party executives, we should consider the possibility that it is an artifact. To explain, assume that a state's elections are entirely determined by the underlying partisan distribution, and the latter is such that any candidate of the majority party has a 60:40 chance of winning. Then, the probability that a minority party candidate will win a governor's race is by definition .4. But the probability that the minority party will win 26 or more seats in a 50-member upper house is a faint .04, and the probability that it will win 101 or more seats in a 200-member lower house is effectively zero.[2] These statistical truisms simply reflect the operation of the law of large numbers: minority control is more likely, the smaller the number of minority successes needed for control. Of course, the proposed null model is not very realistic, but it is sufficient to make the point that there are nonsubstantive reasons for expecting minority party governors as the modal end to unified control.[3]

In light of this fact we need to identify empirical regularities not predicted by an artifactual model before investing much effort in formulating alternative "real" explanations for minority party governorships. Before proceeding to this task, note that an artifactual explanation does not appear to account for the national results.

---

[2]From the normal approximation to the binomial distribution.
[3]This abstract logic no doubt would be reinforced by the minority's recognition of it, which would lead them to concentrate their resources on gubernatorial races.

Since 1952 the Democrats have won an average of 60 percent of the seats in the House of Representatives. If these thousands of outcomes reflected the underlying probability of Democratic victory, then the probability that Republican presidential candidates have simply been on a hot streak since 1952 would be .042 (seven of ten wins, given probability of a win equal to .4)—within the realm of possibility, but not likely.

This latter observation suggests a counter-factual implication of artifactual explanations of the minority-party-governor phenomenon. According to an artifactual explanation, episodes of minority-headed divided government would be occasional and sporadic rather than frequent and persistent, with such episodes being less common and less persistent, the more one-sided a state's partisanship. While the minority party should win an occasional gubernatorial race, its underlying partisan disadvantage should prevent it from retaining the governor's mansion for a long period. Of course, real-world factors like incumbency might make two-term minority governorships reasonably common, but can we find state-level analogies to the national pattern, where, against the odds, the minority party wins the executive more frequently and more persistently than partisanship would suggest? The answer is a clear yes.

There is, of course, North Dakota. The Erikson–McIver–Wright partisanship measure ranks the state eighth in Republican partisanship, but for twenty consecutive years (1960–80) the Democrats held the governorship while the Republicans held the upper house and usually the lower as well. Even if the probability of the North Dakota Democrats' winning any given gubernatorial election were as high as .49, the probability of winning five in a row is $.49^5$, which is less than .03. Kansas is the third most Republican state, and until 1990 it had elected a Democratic lower house only once in the period of this study, but the Democrats have controlled the governorship for twenty-two of thirty-six years between 1946 and 1992. Idaho (second in Republican partisanship) has had a Democratic governor and Republican legislature since 1970, ditto Wyoming (sixth) since 1976. California is an interesting case. From 1940 to 1956 Republicans owned the legislature, from 1958 to 1966 the state was unified Democratic, and since 1966 California's government has resembled the national pattern with sixteen years of Republican governors and Democratic legislatures.

On the other side, the examples are less striking but still plentiful. The Southern states, of course, have the highest Democratic partisanship scores, but in all of the following cases, the Democrats have an advantage in state party identification. Oregon has had a Democratic upper house since 1958, but these Democratic majorities have had to work with Republican governors in twenty-four of thirty-four years. Neighboring Washington has had a Republican governor and Democratic upper house in sixteen of the past twenty-eight years. Delaware and Illinois have had Republican governors and Democratic upper houses since 1976. Missouri has had a Republican governor and Democratic legislature since 1980. Finally, in West Virginia (seventh in Democratic partisanship) the Republicans have not captured either house of the legislature during the period of our study, but they controlled the governorship for sixteen of forty-six years.

In sum, patterns of divided government in the states seem to reflect something more than the random successes of minority party gubernatorial candidates. There appear to be too many such victories, and the resulting strings of divided government seem too long to be explained as the sporadic occurrences of unlikely events. The same is obviously true at the national level. What then?

Balancing Explanations of Divided Government

Until recently analyses of elections for different public offices proceeded in isolation from one another. Presidential elections analyses employed one set of major concepts—parties, issues, ideology, and candidate traits. Congressional elections analyses employed a different set—incumbency, campaign spending, the quality of challengers. The major point of contact between the two areas of work was the notion of presidential coattails: the popularity of presidential candidates and the performance of the incumbent president have some impact on the fortunes of congressional candidates. Numerous studies suggested, however, that this impact had been declining.[4] While this large body of work did not explicitly address the subject of divided government,

---

[4]George C. Edwards, *Presidential Influence in Congress* (San Francisco: Freeman, 1980), 70–78.

the explanation implied by it would simply be that voters vote *differently* for different offices. Research would have offered no specific explanation for opposite patterns in different states, it would only have said that the candidates and what they embodied must have differed in ways sufficient to produce the opposing patterns.

Very recently a number of analysts have proposed what I will term "balancing" explanations of divided government. These explanations presume that some citizens have a general appreciation of the institutional structure of American government and that such institutional considerations enter into their voting decisions. In contrast to the legislative professionalism argument, balancing arguments have an element of purpose or intention in them. To forestall misunderstanding, let me be very clear about this point.

To suggest that some voters make choices that have the consequence of dividing government is not to claim that there are millions of voters walking around saying "I voted for George Bush because I felt he was better than Mike Dukakis, but I voted for a Democratic representative because I wanted to attach a ball and chain to Bush's ankle." It is unlikely that many such voters exist. But voters may be doing something less conscious. Having made a decision to support Bush and feeling less than enthusiastic about it, they may be predisposed to listen to Democratic appeals for other offices. Having tentatively decided to support Richard Nixon or Ronald Reagan and having been nervous about their decision, voters might have been susceptible to the appeals of other Democratic candidates. While not consciously choosing a divided government, people may have a vague appreciation of the overall picture that plays some role in how they vote. People could be voting as if they are making conscious choices to divide government even if their individual decisions are well below the conscious level.

A number of polls have shown that Americans approve of divided government. In an NBC News/*Wall Street Journal* (*WSJ*) survey taken before the 1988 elections, 54 percent of likely voters preferred that different parties control the presidency and Congress while only 32 percent preferred unified government.[5] In an October 1990 NBC/

---

[5]James W. Perry, "United We Stand May Still Be the U.S. Ideal, but Divided We Vote Has Become the Reality," *Wall Street Journal* (14 November 1988): A20.

WSJ survey, the margin of divided government supporters was about 3:1 (67:23 percent).[6] While such sentiments certainly do not imply that so many voters consciously choose divided control, they do indicate that the idea of divided government is sufficiently meaningful that voters do not hesitate to offer an evaluation of one, an evaluation coincidentally consistent with what they collectively choose.[7] That is the notion underlying balance models: the overall pattern of election outcomes is consistent with the notion of an electorate behaving *as if* it were consciously choosing or rejecting divided government.

Model 1: Matching Party and Institutional Strengths

Jacobson's explanation occupies an intermediate position between traditional by-product explanations of divided government and newer, full-fledged balancing arguments. He observes that Americans view the Republican party as superior to the Democrats in the realms of macro-economic management and foreign relations. But they perceive the Democrats as more compassionate and more likely to ensure a fair distribution of national benefits and burdens. Given that the modern presidency is preeminent in the realms of international relations and economic management, while Congress is traditionally concerned with distribution, the present pattern of divided national government fits popular sentiment. Voters match party strengths with institutional responsibilities by giving the presidency to the Republicans and Congress to the Democrats. Essentially, they have the Republicans bake the economic pie (and protect it from marauding bears and other dangers), but allow the Democrats to divide it up. Stated less colloquially, the Republicans deliver allocative efficiency, while the Democrats deliver distributive justice.

Jacobson's argument is quite plausible, and aggregate national survey data are consistent with it, but he does not show that the people who hold the posited perceptions are those most likely to split

---

[6]"Public Scrutiny: Divided Government," *The Public Perspective* 2 (January/February 1991): 86.

[7]A generation ago political analysts made much of the fact that fewer than half the voters knew which party controlled the House before Eisenhower's reelection in 1956. When Nixon was reelected in 1972, fully three-fourths of the voters knew that the Democrats controlled the House. In the interim some learning evidently occurred.

their tickets. And quite plainly, Democratic-headed divided governments in North Dakota, Wyoming, Colorado, and Idaho are beyond the scope of his explanation, unless the electorates of those states have perceptions of party strengths that are quite the opposite of those held by the national electorate.

Model 2: Governmental Degeneration

Consider the Massachusetts elections of 1990. The Massachusetts legislature has been under Democratic control since 1958, but from 1964 to 1974 the Republicans controlled the governorship. In 1974 a Democrat won the governorship, inaugurating a string of sixteen years of unified Democratic government. During the 1980s conditions in the state were so good that the incumbent Democratic governor parlayed the "Massachusetts Miracle" into the presidential nomination of his party. By 1990, however, conditions had deteriorated dramatically. With revenues pouring in during the 1980s there had been little need to set priorities or make hard choices. Moreover, there had been no pressure to address rapidly growing health expenditures. As a result state expenditures ballooned. Signs of trouble were apparent by the late 1980s, but the exigencies of presidential politics led top state officials to discount bad indicators, accept optimistic forecasts, and otherwise postpone the day of reckoning. By 1990 recession had set in; deficits were growing; taxes had been raised twice; the legislature was paralyzed by the need for yet another, larger increase; and the lame duck Democratic governor had become a political pariah.

Feeling misled and manipulated, the population reacted predictably. Levels of distrust and resentment reached startling heights.[8] A draconian tax limitation initiative led in the polls until the general election campaign, when it wilted under a ferocious assault by a united front of the media, public officials, interest groups, and the Catholic Church.

---

[8]In a late summer *Boston Globe* poll, 81 percent of registered voters reported that state government was out of touch, 65 percent were not very confident state government could solve the problems facing it, only 6 percent had more confidence in state government than in any other level, and 48 percent volunteered that state government served "the politicians" (and 5 percent, "nobody"), as opposed to the rich, the poor, or all the people. Scot Lehigh, "Poll Shows Rollback Would Win Decisively," *The Boston Globe* (3 September 1990): 1, 8–9.

The 1990 elections took place against this backdrop of popular frustration. In the September primaries both party-endorsed gubernatorial candidates lost decisively. John Silber, a Texas emigrant who had supported Republican presidents since 1980, won the Democratic primary despite (or because of) a series of "Silber shockers" that insulted the entire range of Democratic constituency groups. Democratic primary voters did not stop there. The party-endorsed Speaker of the assembly was defeated in his attempt to move up to state treasurer. Even the attorney general (former Congressman Jim Shannon) was swept away by the anti-incumbent tide. It is interesting that, while that tide rolled through the ranks of candidates for executive positions, it stopped short of the steps of the legislature. Only a handful of incumbents lost primaries.

In the general election the electorate completed its revenge. Republican William Weld defeated Silber, ending sixteen years of unified Democratic government. A Republican won the patronage-rich treasurer's office for the first time in forty years. Meanwhile, in the legislative elections the Republicans gained seats, but still emerged on the short end of 123–37 (House) and 24–16 (Senate) party divisions.

A disinterested observer watching the Massachusetts campaign could not help being struck by the irony of it all. For twelve of sixteen years the state had been led by a governor of unquestioned personal integrity, considerable intelligence, and alleged administrative skill.[9] Yet a majority of the electorate believed that corruption, incompetence, and mismanagement were rampant in the state.[10]

---

[9]Dukakis was upset in the 1978 primary following his first term. He served as governor again from 1982–90.

[10]To fully appreciate the mood of the electorate, consider that the following remarks appeared in the *sports section* of *The Boston Globe:*

> I am a lifelong Democrat, a lifelong liberal Democrat, never once voting for a Republican for any office, at any level. My father's words are still clear to me, that my arms would fall off the instant I ever pulled a Republican lever, and I need my arms to type. But I am willing to chance dictating the rest of my stories the rest of my days.... In my life I have never been so angry at how the Democratic party has ripped us off, serving only itself and its minions, rotten to its core. And I am a Democrat speaking.

Michael Madden, "Memory of Blocking Northeastern Move Will Not Fade Away," *The Boston Globe* (4 November 1990): 66.

The explanation, I think, lies in Acton's classic dictum that "power tends to corrupt." Consistent with such sentiments, generations of political scientists have noted the salutary effects of two-party competition and the cleansing properties of party alternation in office. In retrospect, Massachusetts provides a nice illustration of this traditional wisdom. After sixteen years of Democratic rule, the statistics suggested that Massachusetts government had grown corpulent.[11] The budget crisis suggested all-around incompetence.[12] There were a few prominent indications of outright corruption.[13] It was time for a change.

How could Massachusetts voters implement such a change? Transforming the partisan composition of the legislature was an impossible task. With 128–31 (House) and 31–9 (Senate) majorities, no one in the state could expect anything but continued Democratic dominance of the legislature. Even if the disparities had been smaller, a major Republican seat gain was never in the cards. Much like U.S. representatives, Massachusetts state legislators maintained close personal ties with their constituents, separated themselves from an unpopular administration, and ducked responsibility as best they could.

While Massachusetts certainly is an extreme case, in general, changing a legislative majority is both difficult and chancy. In the first place there is a coordination problem. Not only must voters defeat the majority party candidate in one district, but also they must do so in coordination with voters in enough other districts to change control of the legislature. Changing legislative control often entails

---

[11]State education expenditures per pupil are among the highest in the nation. The state provides thirty-two of thirty-three optional Medicaid services and is the only state that reimburses providers directly for Medicaid bills. Some voters saw generosity in statistics like these; more saw extravagance, or at least felt unable to afford such generosity.

[12]Immediately following a major tax increase that made the 1990 national budget fight look like an exercise in political leadership, 86 percent of registered voters said that the state budget would continue out of balance (see footnote 8). They were correct.

[13]Between the primaries and the general election, the city's principal newspaper, *The Boston Globe*, ran a damning investigative series on waste, incompetence, and the illegitimate use of political influence in the municipal court system.

changing many majorities. In Massachusetts, for example, Republicans would have had to win fifty Democratic-held districts (of 128) to take control of the lower house.

In the second place, partial success in changing a legislative majority can be costly. If only *your* district changes its party representation, an experienced member of the majority party is replaced by an inexperienced member of the minority party, with a possible loss in constituency service and district benefits. Enough districts must change representation to shift the legislative majority; anything short of that and the changing districts forfeit their legislative influence while receiving no compensation in the form of increased general benefits.[14]

Neither consideration applies to executive offices. Only one majority need be changed to shift control of the governorship. And the question of putting one's district at a disadvantage if control does not change simply does not arise. Thus, voters who want to end unified control will generally find voting for the gubernatorial candidate of the minority party to be the simpler and more efficient way to achieve their aim. The logic resembles that of the classic Prisoner's Dilemma. Stable legislative majorities enable mutually supportive webs of legislators, interest groups, and bureaucrats to form and grow, uninterrupted by political change. To mix metaphors, the ship of state gradually becomes encrusted with barnacles.[15] Eventually, a majority of the electorate comes to believe that the system has been bargained into a suboptimal state, but because of the difficulties of coordinating with other districts, any given district finds it dangerous to defect from the majority party logroll. A minority party governor is the solution to the game.

Of course, the force of the preceding argument will vary with particular features of states. In general, the more entrenched legislative majorities appear to be, the more a popular desire for change will focus on the executive. This argument has at least three testable implications. *Other things being equal*, we would expect the governor

---

[14]Mark Zupan, "An Economic Explanation for the Existence and Nature of Political Ticket Splitting," *Journal of Law and Economics* 34(1991): 343–369.

[15]Mancur Olson, *The Rise and Decline of Nations* (New Haven, CT: Yale University Press, 1982).

Table 5-1   How Unified Governments End

Duration	Lose chamber	Lose governor	Lose both
2–4 years	29	24	6
6–8 years	8	22	1
10–40 years	1	27	0

to be the agent of change (1) the more one-sided are legislative majorities (that is, the more legislators who must be changed) and (2) the longer the duration of majority party legislative control (what has been will continue to be). Some evidence consistent with this second proposition appears in Table 5-1. Unified government episodes of two to four years are more likely to be terminated by changes in legislative majorities than in executive majorities. Beyond four years, however, termination of unified control is very likely to be the result of change in gubernatorial control, and beyond ten years it is almost a certainty that unified control will end via a minority party's gubernatorial victory. Ironically, secure legislative majorities may be an electoral disadvantage for executive candidates of the majority party.[16]

A third testable implication involves the argument about legislative professionalization introduced earlier. Professionalization is an important component of the increased advantage of incumbency in the U.S. House of Representatives. As discussed in Chapter 4, members desirous of reelection and in possession of considerable resources have both the motive and the opportunity to build individual coalitions based on personal contact and district service. The "personal" constituencies they construct help to insulate them from

---

[16]Jumping back to the national level, this argument complements Erikson's delightful thesis that the Democrats deliberately lose the presidency in order to maximize their success in Congress. Equally tongue-in-cheek, my argument implies that Democrats should deliberately lose legislatures if they wish to elect more executives. Robert Erikson, "Why the Democrats Lose Presidential Elections," *PS: Political Science and Politics* 22 (1989): 30–35.

the national forces that play a much larger role in presidential elections. As a general matter, professionalized legislatures are more electorally insulated than less professionalized ones.[17] Thus, we would expect the governor to be the agent of change (refer to preceding paragraph) (3) the more professionalized the state legislature.

Zupan offers a similar but more complex theory that combines ideology with a Prisoner's Dilemma dynamic. He contends that Democratic ideology places more emphasis on local benefits, while Republican ideology places more emphasis on national benefits. Thus, voters who elect Republicans to legislative office forego local benefits. If a majority of other districts are not so self-sacrificing, then the districts that elect Republicans are "suckers" who pay for the local benefits of other districts, but receive none of their own. When it comes to executive office, however, no such considerations apply, and the more that Democratic legislatures have logrolled for local benefits, the more the incentive to support Republican executives.[18]

The logic of my argument resembles Zupan's, though mine does not posit any link between the parties and particular issues or ideologies. One does not need ideology to explain the national and state data. One need posit only that continuous party control results in a build-up of waste, fraud, and abuse (WFA), which eventually leads majorities to opt for change. When that time comes it is generally easier to make the executive the agent of change than the legislature. To be sure, Zupan's model provides another explanation for the Republican disadvantage at the state legislative level, whereas I must offer other explanations (such as increasing professionalization) for that situation. But in turn, Zupan's model provides no explanation at all for Democratic-headed divided government.

Still, no argument is perfectly complete, and the government degeneration theory fails to provide a complete explanation of state election patterns, for it does not really explain why divided government *persists*. That is, periodic minority party gubernatorial victories

---

[17]Asher, "The Unintended Consequences of Legislative Professionalism"; Lawrence C. Dodd and Sean Q. Kelly, "The Electoral Consequences of Presentational Style," presented at the August, 1990 Annual Meeting of the American Political Science Association, San Francisco.

[18]Zupan, "An Economic Explanation."

may be useful instruments for flushing out WFA, but why should divided government become a more or less permanent state of affairs? One answer is that for most voters the policy-making role of state government is sufficiently limited that guarding against WFA is more important than the greater policy-making efficiency that unified government might bring. Another answer is that persistent divided government reflects still another kind of balancing—programmatic or ideological balancing.

Model 3: In Search of Moderation

In an earlier article that addressed divided control during the Reagan administration, I proposed a model of policy or ideological balancing.[19] While this model provides explanations for a wider range of developments than the two balancing models described above, it makes assumptions about voters that are unlikely to be literally satisfied in large numbers. Thus, I emphasize the *as if* character of the model: the electorate in the large seems to behave as if it were balancing the policies or ideologies of the opposing parties by placing them in control of different institutions.

The model is a spatial model; voters and parties are arrayed along a policy or ideological dimension that runs from left to right (Figure 5-2). Such models have been developed by researchers as a way of representing common political discourse. Consider the frequency of spatial metaphors in political discussion—"parties of the left and right," "move to the center," "extreme left," "ultraright," "being outflanked," and so forth.[20] Voters are assumed to have most preferred positions, called "ideal points," and to become progressively less favorable to policies as the policies depart from their ideal in either direction. Parties, in turn, adopt positions in order to

---

[19]"The Reagan Years: Turning to the Right or Groping Toward the Middle?" in Barry Cooper, Allan Kornberg, and William Mishler, *The Resurgence of Conservatism in Anglo-American Democracies* (Durham, NC: Duke University Press, 1988), 430–59.

[20]The seminal work is Anthony Downs, *An Economic Theory of Democracy* (New York: Harper and Row, 1957), chap. 7. For a comprehensive survey of the spatial modelling literature see James Enelow and Melvin Hinich, *The Spatial Theory of Voting* (Cambridge, England: Cambridge University Press, 1984).

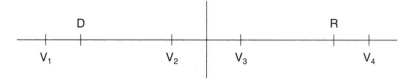

Figure 5-2   Electoral Choice in a Unitary System

appeal to voters and win elections. In Figure 5-2 we array four voters, denoted V_1, V_2, V_3, V_4, from the far left to the far right, and place party D on the left, and party R on the right. The vertical line between V_2 and V_3 is a *cutting line* that separates all voters who are closer to D from those closer to R. If more voters lie to the left of the cutting line than to the right, D wins.

Now, to breathe some life into this abstract representation, imagine that Figure 5-2 represents a hypothetical political system, a system that somewhat resembles—*in greatly simplified form*—the United States circa 1984. This hypothetical system has two parties: the San Francisco Democrats (D) and the Reagan Republicans (R). Neither party is a microcosm of the electorate. When voters look at party D, they see disproportionate numbers of minorities, gay rights activists, radical feminists, and peaceniks; when voters look at party R, they see disproportionate numbers of fundamentalists, bigots, pro-life activists, and chicken-hawks (again, I emphasize that this is a hypothetical situation constructed to allow a clear argument). When the voters compare the policy positions of the two parties, they see distinct differences. On economic policy, the D party favors higher income taxes and more spending on human services on the grounds that most citizens are rich and can easily afford it. On the other hand, the R party favors tax breaks for the rich and reduced human services spending on the grounds that the poor are mostly lazy and undeserving. On foreign policy, the D party says true democracy is found only in certain Third World workers' paradises. In contrast, the R party says nuclear war is really nothing to worry about so long as you have three feet of dirt and a shovel. I could go on in this vein, but I trust the point is clear.

For voter V_1, a liberal activist, party D stands for all that is good and true. Voter V_4, a conservative activist, feels a similar affection toward party R. But voters V_2 and V_3, moderate middle-of-the-road citizens, are much less enthusiastic about their choices. They are tolerant of minority groups and points of view but remain wedded to traditional values. They want low taxes but also a cushion for economic losers. They want an adequate defense but prefer negotiation to confrontation. In a parliamentary system such as that of Great Britain, such moderate voters must like it or lump it; their choices are limited to casting an unenthusiastic vote for the closer party or abstaining.[21] If everyone votes, V_2 votes for D and V_3 for R.

But suppose that our hypothetical political system has a presidential form of government, like the United States, with independent elections for executive and legislative offices. For purposes of simplifying the argument, assume that the legislature is unicameral. Then, the voters in the hypothetical system have the option of voting for unified control of legislative and executive institutions, or of voting for divided control. This means that they can choose among four "platforms" rather than two:

DD: unified D
DR: divided—D executive/R legislature
RD: divided—R executive/D legislature
RR: unified R

Voters understand, of course, that the executive and the legislature together determine public policy, so that when control of the two institutions is divided, any adopted policies must be compromises between the two party's platforms. A common algebraic way of representing such a compromise is by a weighted average:

$$\text{Policy} = q(\text{executive policy}) + (1 - q)(\text{legislative policy})$$
$$(0 < q < 1)$$

The weight, q, represents the power of the executive, and the complementary weight $(1 - q)$ the power of the legislature. If

---

[21]Unless a third party enters the arena, as in fact happened in 1979 when Labour leaders dissatisfied with the drift of their party joined with the Liberals to form the Alliance.

$q = .5$, the executive and legislature are equally powerful, and public policy is a 50:50 mixture of what the two institutions favor. If voters believe that the executive is twice as influential as the legislature in determining policy, then q would be 2/3 and $(1 - q)$ would be 1/3. If the latter situation is the case, then voters in this hypothetical society would face the choices depicted in Figure 5-3 rather than Figure 5-2. DR is the position determined by the equation $(\frac{2}{3}D + \frac{1}{3}R)$, and RD is the position determined by $(\frac{2}{3}R + \frac{1}{3}D)$.

There are now three cutting lines. As before, the middle cutting line separates those voters closer to position DD, a unified Democratic government, from those closer to position RR, a unified Republican government. But two other cutting lines now separate split-ticket voters from straight-ticket voters. Voters between the left and center cutting lines are closest to the DR position (divided government with a Democratic executive and Republican legislature) and will split their tickets accordingly, while voters between the center and right cutting lines are closer to the RD position (divided government with a Republican executive and Democratic legislature) and will split their tickets the opposite way. Given the option of splitting their tickets, V_2 and V_3 are now much happier with their choices.

Depending on voter preferences, divided government can easily result. Figure 5-4 depicts a situation in which 25 percent of the electorate lies in the DD interval (everyone left of the left cutting line). Such voters are closest to DD and cast a straight D ticket. Similarly, 20 percent of the electorate lies in the DR interval, 35 percent in the RD interval, and 20 percent in the RR interval. This electorate casts 55 percent of its vote for the Republican executive candidate (everyone in RD and RR) and 60 percent of its vote for Democratic legislative candidates (everyone in DD and RD).

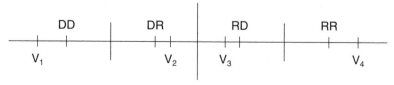

Figure 5-3 Electoral Choice in a Separation-of-Powers System

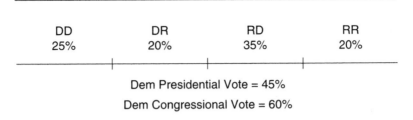

Figure 5-4   Example of Divided Government

In this simple policy-balancing model, ticket-splitters come from the central, moderate range of the ideological spectrum. More extreme voters cast straight tickets, while moderate voters are more likely to split their tickets. Not surprisingly, this happens to be true in recent American elections. In 1984 and 1988, for example, there is a significant relationship between ticket-splitting and placing oneself in the middle ranges of a liberal-conservative scale.[22]

Additional insight can be obtained by examining some dynamics of this simple model. Suppose that at one time competitive pressures have brought the parties very close together, so that many feel there's not a dime's worth of difference between them. Under such conditions, split-ticket voting is minimized, as the left and right cutting lines move very close to the center (Figure 5-5, top). Most voters will fall into either the DD or the RR intervals, where straight-ticket voting is their choice (not that it makes a lot of difference). Now, suppose that factors *other than a shift in voter preferences* lead the parties to polarize. Perhaps dissatisfied activists in the R party come to believe that there is a large conservative population that does not vote out of

[22]Split-ticket voting is significantly associated with moderate ideological positioning and weak partisanship:
1988: Ticsplit = −1.28 + .13 ideology + .20 party ID
          (7.50) (2.39)   (3.82)
1984: Ticsplit = −1.61 + .14 ideology + .24 party ID
          (8.63) (2.54)   (5.82)
(probit estimates, *t*-statistics in parentheses). The seven-point ideology and party identification scales are "folded" so that they run from 1 to 4 (extremist to moderate, strong partisan to pure independent, respectively).

disgust with the lack of choice the parties offer, so the R party moves right to offer the electorate "a choice, not an echo." Perhaps intense disagreement with party policies and the emergence of new social movements lead the D party to move left. In this changed situation there is a significant increase in ticket splitting as the left and right cutting lines move apart (Figure 5-5, bottom).

Is the resemblance of this simple model to recent American electoral history purely coincidental? In 1964 the Goldwater movement captured the Republican party, and in 1968 the Democrats split into new politics and traditionalist wings. During that interval of time, ticket-splitting in presidential–House races jumped 10 percent (Figure 2-1). If polarization of the two parties in fact contributed to the rise in ticket-splitting, as the model suggests, it identifies a striking irony in the efforts of contemporary ideologues. Demanding a choice, not an echo, they pulled their candidates toward more extreme positions. But preferring the echo to the choice, an increasing number of voters split their tickets. Activists tried to impose principled programmatic government; voters responded with divided government.

Can the pattern of split-ticket voting be explained by such a model? Yes, it emerges as a simple function of the weight, q. When

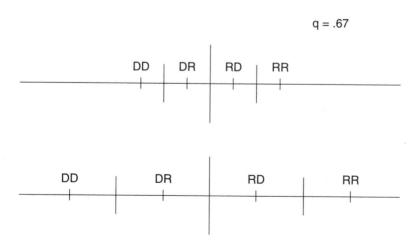

Figure 5-5 Effect of Party Polarization

$q > .5$ (the executive is relatively more influential than the legislature in determining policy), voters will support the executive candidate of the party closer to them on the issues. Certainly, on the national level most analysts have viewed the presidency as stronger than the Congress at least since the time of FDR; thus, ticket-splitting would be composed primarily of Republican president/ Democratic congressional voters when the Republicans are closer to the median voter on the issues than are the Democrats. On first hearing this might seem to contradict the available evidence since there was much discussion of Mondale's being closer to the electorate than Reagan was in 1984. But the Republican *party* was clearly perceived as closer to the median than the Democrats (Table 5-2),

Table 5-2   Voter Policy Positions Compared with Perceptions of Party Positions (Averages on Seven-Point Scales)

	Democratic position	Citizen position	Republican position
Liberal-conservative ideology[a]	3.1	4.3	5.1
Government provision of public services[a]	5.3	3.8	2.9
Aid to minorities[a]	3.0	4.2	4.6
U.S. involvement in Central America	4.5	4.5	3.0
Defense spending	3.2	4.0	5.4
Aid to women[a]	3.1	3.9	4.6
Cooperation with Soviet Union[a]	3.2	4.1	4.9
Government responsibility for jobs and living standards[a]	3.1	4.4	4.9

[a]Republican party closer to mean voter position.
Source: 1984 ANES.

Table 5-3 Voter Policy Positions Compared with Perceptions of Reagan and Mondale Positions, 1984 (Averages on Seven-Point Scales)

Issue	Reagan position	Citizen position	Mondale position
Fewer services or increased spending?	2.74	3.86	5.11
Government should aid minorities, or they should help themselves	4.66	4.08	3.04
Government should guarantee jobs and standard of living, or individual responsibility	5.15	4.34	3.16

Source: 1984 ANES.

and issues on which Mondale was closer, such as the ERA and Central America, were simply not of major concern to voters who were not already Democratic loyalists. There is little doubt that on core issues involving race, taxes, and traditional values, Reagan was closer than Mondale (Table 5-3). More recently, using extensive evidence from the 1988 ANES Senate study, Erikson shows that the Republican party and George Bush were closer to the average voter than the Democratic party and Michael Dukakis, and, more generally, Republican House and Senate candidates on average were perceived as closer to the average voter than their Democratic opponents.[23]

Not only does a policy balancing model explain the national pattern of Republican presidents/Democratic Congresses, but it can explain the unusual state patterns as well. Within the model, Democratic-headed divided government can occur in two ways. The first

[23]Robert Erikson, "Roll Calls, Reputations, and Representation in the U.S. Senate," *Legislative Studies Quarterly* 15 (1990): 630.

is if the Democrats are closer to the electorate on the issues. In that event the national pattern would be reversed. Thinking of the states in which Democratic-headed divided government occurs—North Dakota, Idaho—this possibility seems somewhat unlikely. The second explanation of Democratic-headed divided government lies in the influence parameter, q. If the executive is perceived as *less* influential than the legislature ($q < .5$), contrary to our assumption about the president vis-à-vis Congress, then ticket-splitters vote for the legislative candidate of the closer party and the executive candidate of the farther one. Thus, states with governors who are institutionally weak would produce patterns of ticket-splitting opposite those found in national elections.

In sum, a model of policy balancing has considerable explanatory power when applied to contemporary American electoral history. It can explain differential patterns of ticket-splitting (and divided government) and changes over time in the incidence of ticket-splitting. Though many analysts will view the assumed calculations as beyond the capacity of real-world voters, it would not be the first time that the collective wisdom of the electorate surprised the experts. For too long political scientists have focused on the failings and flaws of the individual citizen. Only recently have we begun to realize that *collectivities* of citizens display an impressive measure of what would be considered rational, responsible behavior. Converse, for example, has observed that, collectively, the citizenry is far more intellectually organized than the *individuals* he studied earlier, a point given theoretical underpinning by Feld and Grofman.[24] And far more extensively, Page and Shapiro show how public opinion—as distinct from the opinions of individual citizens—is coherent and responsive.[25] Perhaps Ladd's reference to divided government as "cognitive Madisonianism" is more than a fanciful metaphor.[26]

[24]Philip E. Converse, "Popular Representation and the Distribution of Information," in John Ferejohn and James Kuklinski, eds., *Information and Democratic Processes* (Chicago: University of Illinois Press, 1990): 369–88; Scott L. Feld and Bernard Grofman, "Ideological Consistency as a Collective Phenomenon," *American Political Science Review* 82 (1988): 773–88.

[25]Benjamin I. Page and Robert Y. Shapiro, *The Rational Public* (Chicago: University of Chicago Press, 1991).

[26]Everett Carll Ladd, "Public Opinion and the 'Congress Problem,'" *The Public Interest* 100 (1990): 66–67.

Probably the most important point to take away from the preceding discussion is the crucial importance of party polarization. When the parties are relatively close, near the center of gravity of the electorate, ticket-splitting declines. When the parties move away from each other, following their own internal dynamics toward the extremes of the voter distribution, they open up a large policy range in which ticket-splitting is the voter response. Small, well-organized cadres of unrepresentative political activists can determine the party positions, but large, unorganized electorates can prevent such positions from being implemented.

Afterthought Revisited: The Puzzle of Senate Elections

Readers who are in a receptive frame of mind may be interested in learning how a policy-balancing model can help explain the puzzling rise in split Senate delegations, noted at the end of Chapter 3. Senate elections are unusual in that from the standpoint of the voter the elections occur in double-member districts. From the standpoint of the sitting senator, however, they are ordinary first-past-the-post elections in single-member districts: the senators never face each other as opponents. From the voter's standpoint Senate elections can produce three possible outcomes: two Democrats, two Republicans, or one of each. But the voter can never express a preference among all three outcomes because in any given election one senator is not running. Thus, the voters have a choice only between two senators of the same party as the senator who is not running, or of one senator from each party. This restriction on voter choice may have interesting consequences.

In an ordinary spatial model of a two-candidate election, the voters simply vote for the candidate closer to them, and the candidate closer to the median wins (Figure 5-6, top panel).[27] But in a Senate election, the voters may very well care about the total repre-

[27]The position of the median voter is the equilibrium position in such models. The median and everyone to the left (by definition of the median, a majority) will oppose any position to the right of the median; conversely, the median and everyone to the right will oppose any position to the left of the median.

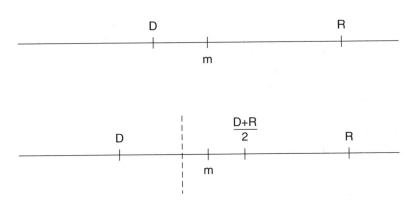

Figure 5-6   The Logic of Split, Polarized Delegations

sentation of their state in the Senate. What if the Democratic candidate is slightly closer to the median voter than the Republican candidate, but the nonrunning senator is a Democrat? Will the median voter still vote for the Democrat if such a vote implicitly means registering a preference for *two* Democratic senators?

If voters care about the total representation of their state, they may very well vote for candidates who are farther from them than their opponents. One algebraic way of representing the total representation of the state in the Senate is via the arithmetic average of their positions. In the bottom panel of Figure 5-6 the Democratic position is closer to the median than the Republican position, but the average of the Democratic and Republican positions is closer still. Thus, with a nonrunning Democratic senator, there will be a tendency to lean toward the Republican candidate, even if farther from the center than the Democrat, since election of the Republican would mean that on average the Senate delegation was closer to the state's median voter than election of a second Democrat. Put simply, the senator who is not running may create an electoral disadvantage for the candidate of her party who is.

Under what conditions does a state elect two senators of the same party? If *both* parties are to the right (or left) of the median voter, two senators of the closer party will represent the state

(Figure 5-7, top panel). If the parties are polarized, but one stays relatively much closer to the median than the other, their average will still be farther from the median than would the position resulting from the election of two senators of the same party (Figure 5-7, bottom panel). Party polarization as in Figure 5-6 is a *necessary* condition for split Senate delegations, but not a sufficient condition. If the parties "bracket" the median voter, and one party is not relatively much farther away from the median than the other, a divided delegation will be chosen.

The preceding logic has been developed in detail elsewhere, and we have conducted a preliminary test on U.S. Senate election results since 1946.[28] Since there is no way of determining the positions of the candidates relative to the median voters in their states, our results are watered down by the inclusion of elections that do not fit the theoretical conditions for splitting seats between the parties. Nevertheless, controlling for incumbency, national trends, and other relevant factors, we found a significant same-party disadvantage in the election returns: for every percent of the vote received by the winning candidate in the preceding election, the incumbent candidate of the same party was penalized almost one-fifth of a vote in the

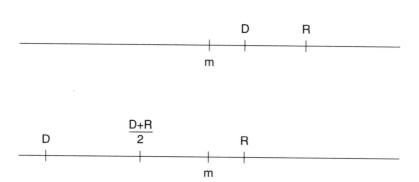

Figure 5-7   The Logic of Unified Delegations

[28]Alberto Alesina, Morris Fiorina, and Howard Rosenthal, "Why Are There So Many Divided Senate Delegations?" National Bureau of Economic Research Working Paper No. 3663, March 1991.

succeeding election. It is too early to say that a balance model such as ours is the explanation of split Senate delegations, but the promise is evident.

Summary

As we saw in Chapters 2 and 3, divided government is a more complex phenomenon than many discussions presume. Once we look at the states as well as the nation, the asymmetric patterns of ticket-splitting and party control, and the persistence of particular forms of divided government, it becomes obvious that multiple causes are at work. To some degree the increased incidence of divided control probably is "accidental," a by-product of such things as party decline, the development of legislative professionalism, and Democratic splits over value-laden social issues. But the patterns of divided control that exist in this country seem to suggest something more as well; namely, that there is some method in the electorate's seeming madness. Some of the aggregate features of election results are consistent with the notion that electorates want the kind of government they have and may even be voting in such a way as to produce it. If there is any validity to such suspicions, then normative discussions of the consequences of divided government are overlooking a critical ingredient. This topic is now ripe for us to address.

CHAPTER 6

The Consequences of Divided Government

For some commentators the consequences of divided government are all too obvious. As they see it, the more or less self-evident negative effects of divided control fall under two general headings. First, divided control exacerbates problems of efficiency and effectiveness that are inherent in the constitutional fabric. Put simply, divided government threatens to make an inefficient form of government unworkable. Second, divided control obscures the accountability of government officials for policies adopted and outcomes realized during their tenure. Responsibility is inherently problematic in a polity with weak parties and a separation of powers, but split control can obscure responsibility altogether.

Although these two concerns resonate with traditional thinking about American politics, a survey of the relevant research indicates that evaluations of divided government have far outrun the empirical evidence on its consequences. Moreover, there has been virtually no attention paid to the question of whether those consequences, even if negative, are worse than those that would ensue if unified control were somehow achieved in the contemporary context. Where one stands on that question hinges critically on why one thinks that divided government has become the norm.

Efficiency and Effectiveness
under Divided Government

In a thoughtful essay, James Sundquist reflects on the contemporary condition of divided national government, contrasting it unfavorably with a unified government model that presupposes an active president supported by cohesive legislative majorities.[1] Generations of scholars have observed that with a system of separated institutions, sharing powers that are intricately blended among them, efficiency has never been a strong point of American democracy. What has made the system workable in the past, so the traditional model asserts, is the unifying force of political party. But the development of a persistent condition of divided government vitiates the critical coordinating force of party. Institutional rivalries now are buttressed by partisan rivalry and partisan electoral interest. One would like to believe that the Tom Foleys, George Mitchells, and George Bushes sit down after elections and say, "Well, now that that's over, let's put our differences aside and do what's best for the country," but such expectations are the stuff of fairy tales, not real politics. As Sundquist observes, the congressional majority has every incentive to reject presidential initiatives; to accept them is to acknowledge the president's competence and sagacity, hence, to support his re-election. Similarly, the president cannot run against Congress in the next election if he admits that congressional initiatives are meritorious. Divided control gives each branch of government an electoral incentive to work for the failure of the branch held by the other.[2]

Thus, it is alleged that problems like the budget and trade deficits fester, foreign policy toward Central America degenerates into bitter partisan stalemate, frustrated presidents go outside normal governmental channels (and the law) in order to achieve their aims, frustrated members of Congress leak secrets and conduct destructive investigations in order to achieve theirs, and government degenerates into a snakepit of no-holds-barred partisan struggles.[3] The normal obstacles of the separation of powers are reinforced many-fold by split control of the separate institutions. Consequently, governing becomes a matter of posturing for the most part, and when actions must be taken, they tend to reflect the least common denominator and satisfy no one. The country suffers as costs mount and opportu-

---

[1]James Sundquist, "Needed: A Political Theory for the New Era of Coalition Government in the United States," *Political Science Quarterly* 103 (1988): 613–35.
[2]Ibid., 629–30.
[3]Benjamin Ginsburg and Martin Shefter, *Politics by Other Means* (New York: Basic Books, 1990), passim.

nities fade because the divided government is incapable of formulating and implementing coherent policies.

Sounds pretty convincing. But unfortunately for proponents of such arguments, there is little research that backs up such strong claims. On the contrary, a small but growing body of research on the effects of divided government indicates that the consequences of split control are not nearly so obvious as the critics assert.

Activist Government

The writings of Cutler, Sundquist, and other critics of divided government reveal a preference for government action. They evidently prefer a government that acts in opposition to their views to one that does not act at all. These commentators see little but drift and stalemate under divided governments and draw unfavorable comparisons between such episodes and other periods when energetic presidents and their legislative majorities adopt major policy initiatives. The critics' arguments are plausible and their examples striking, but often in social science striking examples are not representative of the larger universe of cases. In this instance a look at that larger universe suggests that divided governments are, on average, no less activist than unified governments.

In the most comprehensive study yet undertaken, David Mayhew finds nothing in the historical record to suggest that periods of divided government are any less productive than periods of unified control. In an exhaustive review of the post-World War II federal record, Mayhew finds that unified governments were no more likely to produce "significant" legislation than were divided governments. Rather, "if all 267 laws are counted equally, the nine 'unified' two-year segments average 12.8 acts, and the 13 'divided' segments average 11.7. The difference is trivial, and since the 1980s was all 'divided,' that decade's shift to the use of omnibus budgetary measures can probably account for it, so to speak, entirely."[4] In light of Mayhew's findings, one won-

---

[4]"Significant" legislation was identified by laborious searches of contemporaneous newspaper accounts (principally *New York Times* and *Washington Post*) of congressional accomplishments and retrospective judgments in policy studies about legislative milestones. See David Mayhew, *Divided We Govern: Party Control, Lawmaking, and Investigations, 1946–1990* (New Haven, CT: Yale University Press, 1991). Mayhew discusses his procedures in Chapter 3. The quotation is from p. 76.

ders what universe of cases Cutler was examining when he claimed that "almost every important domestic program in this country that has been carried through the Congress has been carried through at a time of party government rather than divided government ."[5]

Additionally, Mayhew finds that divided control does not lead to more significant instances of congressional investigation/harassment of the executive. Indeed, some of the most far-reaching and damaging investigations (such as those of Senator Joe McCarthy) took place under unified governments. Contemporary commentators may overemphasize the Watergate experience while overlooking the post-World War II Red scare: the congressional hearings on internal subversion that began in 1948 and extended to 1954 took place mostly under unified control. Mayhew finds that fifteen major investigations took place during the eighteen years of unified control, while fourteen major investigations took place during the twenty years of divided control, hardly the kind of picture the charges of some commentators would lead us to expect.[6]

While extremely suggestive, Mayhew's findings will not completely convince the critics of divided government. For one thing, Mayhew does not attempt to gauge the worth or effectiveness of the legislation. Thus, "good" legislation produced by a unified government could be weighted the same as "poor" legislation produced by a divided government, so long as both are judged to be significant pieces of legislation. For example, consider the contemporary savings and loan (S & L) debacle. Mayhew counts the Garn–St. Germain Depository Institutions Act (1982), which has been roundly condemned as contributing to the debacle, as a major piece of legislation.[7] But should anyone object to that judgment, Mayhew replies that if the critics would discount such measures, they should likewise discount the Depository Institutions and Monetary Control Act of

[5]Lloyd N. Cutler, "Some Reflections About Divided Government," *Presidential Studies Quarterly* 17 (1988): 490.
[6]Mayhew defines a major investigation as one revolving around a committee-based charge (or response thereto) of misbehavior by the executive branch that receives front page coverage by the *New York Times* on at least twenty days. Mayhew, *Divided We Govern*, 9–10.
[7]The act "unleashed" S & Ls, allowing them to enter areas of business previously closed to them.

1980, which raised the ceiling on the interest rates thrifts could offer and raised federal deposit insurance from $40,000 to $100,000, another piece of legislation that clearly contributed to the S & L debacle. Evidently, divided governments have no monopoly on "bad" legislation.[8]

Even if we could measure the appropriateness of legislative response to everyone's satisfaction and still found that unified and divided governments were equally efficacious in that sense, an irreducible ambiguity in Mayhew's findings would still remain. Essentially, he has studied the *supply* of federal legislation and found that the supply is more or less the same during modern unified and divided government periods. But we have no information about the *demand* for legislation. If unified and divided government periods are characterized by different levels of demand, then they would need to supply different amounts of legislation in order to be operating equally well. Recall that Table 2-2 shows that divided government occurs during some of the more troubled eras of our political history. If such eras demand more by way of government response than unified eras, supplying only the same amount of response as that supplied in unified eras would indicate that the government response is unsatisfactory relative to that in unified eras. While this argument is plausible, critics of divided government cannot take a great deal of comfort in it, for one could also argue the opposite point of view: if divided government reflects a lack of consensus in the society, then perhaps government should supply *less* rather than more legislation in divided periods than in more consensual unified periods.

It is doubtful that much progress can be made on the questions just raised. Economic historians continue to debate the wisdom or lack thereof of federal laws a century after they were passed.[9] More-

---

[8]Mayhew wryly observes that a unified government was responsible for the Smoot-Hawley tariff (1930), "which, from the standpoint of the world economy, may have been the most unfortunate statute enacted by the U.S. government during the 20th Century." *Divided We Govern*, 189, n. 39.

[9]For different evaluations of the Interstate Commerce Act of 1887, see R. M. Spann and E. W. Erickson, "The Economics of Railroading: The Beginning of Cartelization and Regulation," *Bell Journal of Economics and Management Science* 1 (1970): 227–44; R. O. Zerbe, Jr., "The Costs and Benefits of Early Regulation of the Railroads," *Bell Journal of Economics* 11 (1980): 343–50.

over, there seems to be no precise way of measuring such a nebulous concept as the "demand for legislation." Mayhew's ambitious study is as careful and thorough a piece of work as can be done. Because of the considerations raised, it may not refute the claims of Sundquist and others once and for all, but at the very least it suggests that their claims are considerably exaggerated and perhaps much more problematic than they appear.

Moreover, once we leave the realm of exhaustive analysis, we can counter the claims of divided government critics with their own ammunition: striking examples. Via examples, one can argue that under certain conditions divided control is more likely to produce legislation. The expansion of Social Security benefits and coverage in the early 1970s was stimulated by the competition for credit between President Nixon and the Democratic Congress.[10] Similarly, the Clean Air Act of 1970 emerged stronger than anticipated because of the one-upsmanship that went on between President Nixon and Democratic Presidential aspirant Senator Edmund Muskie, the responsible committee chair.[11] The Economic Recovery Tax Act of 1981 was the result of a bidding war between President Reagan and House Democrats.[12] Sure, it was lousy public policy, but if it's action you want, divided government provided it. On a more positive front, the passage of the 1986 Tax Reform Act is widely applauded and not well understood, but at least part of the explanation seems to be that neither party wished to bear the blame for allowing the legislation to fail.[13] It is tempting to conclude that when a popular consensus behind public policy exists, divided government will not stand in its way; it may even facilitate action. While neither party can accomplish everything it wants to in divided government periods, the struggle for political credit sometimes makes both parties as likely to compromise behind some legislation as to allow the process to stalemate. Some

---

[10]R. Kent Weaver, *Automatic Government* (Washington, DC: Brookings, 1988): chap. 4.

[11]Charles O. Jones, *Clean Air: The Policies and Politics of Pollution Control* (Pittsburgh, University of Pittsburgh Press, 1975), chap. 7.

[12]David Stockman, *The Triumph of Politics* (New York: Avon, 1986).

[13]Timothy J. Conlan, Margaret T. Wrightson, and David R. Beam, *Taxing Choices: The Politics of Tax Reform* (Washington, DC: Congressional Quarterly Press, 1990), 70–71, 89–90, 158.

partisan compromises are indisputably bad policy, as was the 1981 tax cut, but but are all the partisan compromises that take place under divided governments bad? Are the policies produced by unified governments invariably good? Is it better to have unified governments and sharp alternations of policies, as when the British Labour party nationalized the steel industry after World War II only to have the Conservative party promptly denationalize it after coming to power? These are not easy questions. Reasonable people certainly may disagree about the answers.

Budget Deficits

According to Lloyd Cutler,

> In modern times high deficits have occurred only with divided government. Economists generally accept that three percent or more of the GNP is the telltale sign of an unacceptably high deficit. We have had ten such deficits since World War II. *Every single one* occurred during a time of divided government—Truman's in fiscal 1948, Ford's in 1975 and 1976, and Reagan's seven in 1982 through 1988. The correlation between unacceptably high deficits and divided government is much too exact to be a coincidence.[14] (emphasis in original)

Cutler chooses his qualifiers carefully. Anyone familiar with American economic history immediately sees the significance of the phrase "in modern times." During the late-nineteenth-century era of divided government, budget *surpluses* were the rule, and were widely viewed as a major problem.[15] Still, a sympathetic reading of Cutler could generalize his logic to cover that counterexample. He asserts that "High deficits occur when the President and Congress cannot form a consensus on a mix of taxes and competing expenditure programs that will create a reasonable balance between inflows

[14]Lloyd Cutler, "Now Is the Time for All Good Men," *William and Mary Law Review* 30 (1989): 391.

[15]Today's readers may have difficult understanding why surpluses should be considered a problem. Briefly, with tariffs providing the bulk of federal revenues, the prices faced by consumers were kept artificially high, even though there was no revenue basis for doing so. Second, surplus revenues naturally generated pressures to spend them, contrary to the views of those favoring a minimal federal role.

and outflows.[16] Substitute "high surpluses" for "high deficits"and the assertion is equally plausible. If the president and Congress cannot reach agreement, then inflows and outflows will be out of balance, but *either* deficit or surplus is a possibility, depending on other factors such as the overall state of the economy.

The qualifier "three percent or more of the GNP" is also important for Cutler's argument. For in fifty of the last sixty years, through unified governments and divided governments alike, expenditures have exceeded revenues.[17] But here again, a sympathetic reading of Cutler could argue that the peacetime deficits of the 1980s are unprecedented in their magnitude and that they are a reflection of divided control.

There is one academic study consistent with this more restricted version of Cutler's claim (that divided control produced exceptionally big deficits in the 1980s), though that study assumes a different conception of divided control than does Cutler. McCubbins argues that split control of Congress (Democratic House, Republican Senate) between 1981 and 1987 generated the unusual peacetime deficits. His argument sees the deficits as the product of the interaction between party preferences and split control.

Assume that the Democrats and Republicans have the following preference orderings for government spending:

Democrats	Republicans
Cut defense, raise domestic	Cut domestic, raise defense
Raise both	Raise both
Cut both	Cut both
Cut domestic, raise defense	Cut defense, raise domestic

If the Democrats control the House of Representatives and the Republicans the Senate, as was the case from 1981 to 1987, then

[16]Cutler, "Now Is the Time for All Good Men," 390.
[17]Matthew McCubbins, "Party Governance and U.S. Budget Deficits: Divided Government and Fiscal Stalemate," in Alberto Alesina and Geoffery Carliner, eds., *Politics and Economics in the 1980s* (Chicago: University of Chicago Press, 1991), 83–111.

neither party can achieve its first preference, since it will be blocked by the other. If the parties deadlock, Congress typically adopts a continuing resolution that provides for funding programs at the previous year's level; given inflation, this is in effect a cut in all programs—the third preference of both parties. Thus, there is an obvious compromise: the parties agree on their second preferences and raise spending across the board. Now, if revenues were to keep pace with expenditures, deficits would not result, but McCubbins argues that in 1981 congressional Republicans and Southern Democrats joined to support the Reagan tax cuts; hence, the deficits.

Clearly, McCubbins's argument has some relevance to the particular events of the 1980s; indeed, it is largely an abstraction of the events that occurred. The question is whether the argument has more general application to American history. Alt and Stewart report results that undercut the generality of arguments derived from the 1980s experience. Looking at the entire statistical history of federal spending, revenues, and deficits/surpluses, they find little evidence that either split control of Congress or split control of Congress and the presidency produces budget deficits. They do find that divided governments seem unable to deal successfully with *ongoing* deficits and surpluses, but divided governments do not seem to generate out-of-balance budgets more than unified governments.[18]

From a logical standpoint, there are other problems with putting so much weight on the events of the 1980s. For one thing, McCubbins' argument depends crucially on the assumption that both parties would have preferred to raise spending across the board than to have seen spending cut across the board. If these two preferences had been reversed, then split party control of the Senate and House would have led to a compromise in which spending was cut across the board. McCubbins may well have party preferences right for the 1980s, but preferences may differ in other eras, past and future, and if so, would have different budgetary consequences.

Finally, let us work through a simple counter-factual exercise; namely, let us ask ourselves what would have happened in the 1980s

---

[18]James Alt and Charles Stewart, "Parties and the Deficit: Some Historical Evidence." Presented at the National Bureau of Economic Research Conference on Political Economics, February 2–3, 1990.

had the Republicans captured both houses of Congress in 1980 and held them for the entirety of Reagan's term. Would the deficits have been smaller than they turned out to be? Republican apologists for the deficits blame Congress for blocking the president's attempts to control domestic expenditures, while Democratic critics charge that the president simply went wild on defense spending and believed the siren's call of supply side tax cuts. What would have happened to each of these three components of the deficit had the government been unified Republican? It seems very likely that defense spending would have risen even more than it did, since the Democratic majorities in the House resisted the president's requests for big increases and finally brought defense increases to a halt in the late 1980s. Similarly, it seems very likely that Republican majorities in Congress would have given the president at least as much in tax cuts as the split Congress did. Thus, two components of the deficits would likely have been *larger* under unified Republican government. The question, then, is whether Republican Congresses would have slashed domestic spending sufficiently to make up for the hypothesized increases in defense spending and tax cuts. The events of 1981–82 suggest not. When faced with the tough decisions to make further cuts in domestic spending, the Republican "gypsy moths" bailed out, essentially blocking that part of the Reagan revolution.[19] Thus, a plausible argument can be made that unified Republican government in the 1980s might have led to even *larger* deficits than those that developed under divided government. Of course, it may be that a unified government would have come to grips with the problem earlier, because of the realization that the Republican party was clearly responsible for the problem. But there is no evidence as yet that the deficits are a major political (i.e., voting) issue, so it is possible that Republican majorities would have been about as unlikely to make tough fiscal and budgetary decisions as split majorities.

In sum, divided control of political institutions probably makes it more difficult for Congress and the president to reach cordial agree-

---

[19]For a recounting of the grinding down of the early 1980s' Reagan blitzkrieg, see David Brady and Morris Fiorina, "The Ruptured Legacy: Presidential-Congressional Relations in Historical Perspective," in Larry Berman, ed., *Looking Back on the Reagan Presidency* (Baltimore: John Hopkins University Press, 1990): 270–76.

ment on a package of expenditure and revenue proposals that would produce a balanced budget (on paper). But whether a deficit results if no such cordial agreement is reached is another question. If revenues are pouring in, as in the late nineteenth century, then surpluses may be the problem, not deficits. And if each party would rather hurt the other's constituencies than help its own, deficits need not result. In each case, as well as others not yet identified, it is not divided control in and of itself, but divided control in conjunction with other important considerations, that produces fiscal problems.[20]

Executive-Legislative Relations

It seems perfectly logical to suppose that divided control would make it more difficult for presidents to work with Congress. Congressional majorities will disagree with the president's policy goals, and this policy and partisan disagreement will reinforce institutional rivalries rooted in the Constitution. The policy-making process will be more conflictual, and the president will be less successful in getting what he wants, beginning with the appointment of like-minded supporters to federal office.

Confirmations

Does split control of the presidency and the Senate make it more difficult for a president to gain confirmation of appointments? Mature readers may recall the Senate battles over President Nixon's attempts to elevate judges Clement Haynesworth and G. Harold Carswell to the Supreme Court. And even the youngest readers should recall the political war precipitated by President Reagan's effort to elevate Robert Bork to the high Court. Similarly, readers will recall the Democratic Senate's savaging of former Republican

---

[20]Palozzo's careful consideration of budgetary politics from 1974 to 1990 comes to exactly this conclusion. He finds that divided government was only one of a number of factors—short- and long-term—that shaped the budgetary conflicts and stalemates of the era. Daniel J. Palozzo, "Budget Politics in the Post-Reform Era: The Separated President Confronts the Stubborn Congress," paper presented at the Carl Albert Center Conference, "Back to the Future: The United States Congress in the Twenty-First Century," April 11–13, 1990, Norman, Oklahoma.

Senator John Tower when President Bush nominated him for Secretary of Defense. Of course, contrary examples also come to mind: a Democratic Senate rejected Lyndon Johnson's nomination of his long-time associate, Abe Fortas, for Chief Justice. When we move beyond striking examples to the full body of evidence, what effects of divided government, if any, appear?

Taking judicial nominations first, it is uncertain whether the president's nominations face tougher sledding when the Senate shares his or her partisan complexion. Lemieux and Stewart find that in the nineteenth century opposition Senates significantly constrained the ability of presidents to put their people on the Supreme Court.[21] In more recent times, however, the little data we have do not suggest much one way or the other.[22] Inclusive of Justice Thomas, Presidents have named twenty-four justices since World War II, nine in unified government years and fifteen in divided years. Four nominations offered during times of divided control were unsuccessful (two rejected under Nixon, one rejected, and one withdrawn under Reagan), as compared with two offered during times of unified control (two withdrawn under Johnson). There is a much larger category of federal district and circuit court judges, but I have been unable to locate tallies of nominations and their fates.

As for nominations to executive offices, the available data do not indicate that failure to control the Senate hurts the chances of presidential nominees. No president since FDR has had more than a half dozen proposed appointees rejected outright, and none since Hoover has been forced to withdraw more than 1 percent of the nominations. Much more often, Senate committees simply fail to report. Table 6-1 presents the failure-to-confirm rate of each Senate since the first election of FDR.

---

[21]Peter Lemieux and Charles Stewart, "A Theory of Supreme Court Nominations," presented at the Conference on Political Economy, National Bureau of Economic Research, December 7–8, 1990, Cambridge, MA.

[22]Cameron, Cover, and Segal have conducted a detailed analysis of individual senator's votes on Supreme Court nominees from Earl Warren to Anthony Kennedy. They find that senators of the president's party are significantly more likely to support his nominees, and that senators are more likely to support nominees when a majority of the Senate shares the president's party. Unfortunately, these findings do not readily translate into estimates of whether divided control makes a difference for whether nominations actually succeed or fail. See Charles M. Cameron, Albert D. Cover, and Jeffrey A. Segal, "Senate Voting on Supreme Court Nominees: A Neoinstitutional Model," *American Political Science Review* 84 (1990): 525–34.

Table 6-1   Senate Action on Presidential Appointments

Congress	Senate control	Total appointments	% Not confirmed
1933–34	Same	9,094	1
1935–36	Same	22,487	1
1937–38	Same	15,330	1
1939–41	Same	29,072	<1
1941–42	Same	24,344	1
1943–44	Same	21,775	2
1945–46	Same	37,022	1
1947–48	Different	66,641	18
1949–51	Same	87,266	1
1951–52	Same	46,920	1
1953–54	Same	69,458	1
1955–56	Different	84,173	2
1957–58	Different	104,193	1
1959–60	Different	91,476	2
1961–62	Same	102,849	2
1963–64	Same	122,190	2
1965–66	Same	123,019	2
1967–68	Same	120,231	2
1969–71	Different	134,464	<1
1971–72	Different	117,053	2
1973–74	Different	134,384	2
1975–76	Different	132,151	3
1977–78	Same	137,504	9
1979–80	Same	154,797	1
1981–82	Same	186,264	1
1983–84	Same	97,893	1
1985–86	Same	99,614	4
1987–88	Different	89,193	7

Source: Harold W. Stanley and Richard G. Niemi, *Vital Statistics on American Politics*, 2nd ed. (Washington, D.C.: CQ Press, 1990), Tables 8–14.

One entry in the table truly stands out: the Republican Senate of 1947–48 (part of the "do-nothing eightieth Congress") showed no great enthusiasm for President Truman's appointees, perhaps anticipating (erroneously) taking control of the presidency in 1948. On the other hand, the next least successful president was Jimmy Carter, who had a 3–2 Senate majority. Republican Richard Nixon was treated rather well by the Democratic Senate of 1969–70, while Reagan was not treated particularly well by the Republican Senate of 1985–86—although it treated him better than did the Democratic Senate two years later. The average success of presidents with congenial Senates is 98 percent, as compared to the 96 percent rate of presidents with opposing Senates, the difference being due mainly to the Truman observation. Perhaps of greater interest, in the two years before a presidential election, presidents facing opposing Senates are successful only 94 percent of the time, as opposed to 98 percent at all other times—opposing Senates may drag their feet in anticipation of their party's winning the presidency. But once again, without the Truman observation, the difference would be trivial.

So, there may be some small degree of increased conflict over presidential appointments when different parties control the presidency and the Senate, and the president may be marginally less successful than when the Senate is organized by his party. But in the interest of even-handedness we should ask whether any added conflict over presidential appointments created by divided government has a positive as well as a negative side. If, under unified government, Congress rubber-stamps presidential appointments, then divided government may provide a welcome dose of increased scrutiny. Is it so obviously wrong to reject a hard drinker for Secretary of Defense, a post that would make him a principal advisor to a president regarding actions that would involve the lives of young American men and women? If unified government would have confirmed Tower, perhaps that is an argument *against* unified government rather than an argument for it. The Supreme Court is a political institution, despite the mythology maintained by legal scholars and recited by self-serving politicians. If the partisan impulses generated by divided government result in the appointment of somewhat more centrist, less ideologically committed justices, is that necessarily bad? To foreshadow a general answer to be offered in the conclusion, it would seem to depend on *why* government is divided. If divided government is an accident, as Sundquist, Cutler, and others assume, then the failure of a president to secure his or her appointees is a negative, pure and simple. But to the extent that divided government reflects any purposeful motivation on the part of voters, constraints on the president's appointment powers would seem to be consistent with that motivation.

Treaties
Just as divided government would seem to create difficulties for presidents seeking to staff the bureaucracy and the courts with like-minded appointments, so it would seem to create analogous difficulties for presidential conduct of international affairs. Article II, Section 1 of the Constitution states that the president "shall have Power, by and with the Advice and Consent of the Senate, to make Treaties, provided two-thirds of the Senators present concur." Thus, one might expect that instances of divided control that place the Senate and presidency in the hands of opposing parties are periods of presidential frustration. Once again, however, the evidence is meager.

Table 6-2 lists the rates at which the Senate has approved the treaties, conventions, and protocols negotiated by post-World War II presidents.[23] As seen, presidents are successful 90 percent or more of the time, with little indication that common party control of the Senate and presidency has any bearing on their success. The most successful administrations were Carter's (unified), the Nixon/Ford combination (split), and Reagan's second (unified two years, and split two years), trailed closely by Nixon's (split), Eisenhower's first (unified two years and split two years), and Johnson's (unified). The least successful administrations were Eisenhower's second (split) and Truman's (unified). Of the thirty-six instances in which the president withdrew his submission or the Senate rejected it outright, twenty-five occurred in the twenty-two unified years, while eleven occurred

---

[23]"Conventions, protocols, and treaties are different names for the same thing, and all are often classified as 'treaties.'...Whether a document is termed a convention, a protocol, or a treaty, it must be submitted to the Senate for ratification." Gary King and Lyn Ragsdale, *The Elusive Executive* (Washington, DC: CQ Press, 1988), 110.

Table 6-2   Divided Control and Senate Approval of Treaties, Conventions, and Protocols

Administration	President/Senate		Approval rate	
Truman	D	D	85%	(74)
Eisenhower I	R	R	97	(32)
	R	D	97	(33)
Eisenhower II	R	D	80	(45)
Kennedy/Johnson	D	D	91	(43)
Johnson	D	D	96	(57)
Nixon	R	D	98	(48)
Nixon/Ford	R	D	100	(60)
Carter	D	D	100	(50)
Reagan I	R	R	91	(81)
Reagan II	R	R	100	(19)
	R	D	100	(22)

Source: Adapted from King and Ragsdale, *The Elusive Executive,* Table 3.4 (updated).

in the fourteen split years—a *higher* rate in unified years than in split years, though not enough to make anything of one way or the other.

Of course, such figures do not incorporate the possibility of rational expectations: expecting difficulties in an opposition-controlled Senate, a president may not send up controversial treaties. Thus, similar success rates in unified and divided regimes could reflect successes with "major" negotiations in the unified case and successes with "minor" negotiations in the divided case. Such strategic considerations almost certainly operate to some degree, but it is difficult to gauge how much.

One argument that has been advanced by the CCS is that anticipating difficulties because of divided control, contemporary presidents eschew the submission of treaties and make more use of executive orders that require no Senate approval. As Petracca, Bailey, and Smith have noted, there is little evidence to support such a claim. Table 6-3 lists the treaties submitted and executive agreements signed during each of the post-World War II presidencies, along with whether the Senate and presidency were in common partisan hands. It is difficult to see any impact of divided government in the figures. Simple linear regressions on the underlying data show a slight upward trend in the use of agreements and a slight downward trend in the use of treaties, which combined yield a significant temporal increase in the *ratio* of agreements to treaties. But that ratio is not related to the presence or absence of a friendly Senate—it peaks in the Johnson and first Reagan administrations (both of which had friendly Senates) and is relatively low during the Nixon administration (unfriendly Senate). Apparently factors other than an opposition Senate lead presidents to utilize agreements rather than treaties.

There is, of course, at least one specific reason that we should not expect divided government to have much impact on the probability that the Senate approves presidential appointments and treaty submissions. That reason is simply that approval requires a two-thirds majority, which one party rarely achieves—since World War II one party has achieved a two-thirds majority only in 1962 and 1964. Thus, presidents seldom can rely solely on their own party in

Table 6-3   Divided Control and Use of Executive Agreements
versus Treaties

Administration	President/ Senate		Treaties	Agreements
FDR/Truman	D	D	24	264
	D	R	39	376
Truman	D	D	12	766
Eisenhower I	R	R	9	332
	R	D	6	525
Eisenhower II	R	D	26	848
Kennedy/Johnson	D	D	32	973
Johnson	D	D	7	798
Nixon	D	R	15	797
Nixon/Ford	D	R	12	996
Carter	D	D	17	1021
Reagan I	R	R	3	739

Source: Adapted from King and Ragsdale, *The Elusive Executive*, Table 3.2 (updated).

the Senate; they generally need some cooperation from the opposing party. Split control implies that more opposition votes are needed, but the condition differs from unified control in degree, not in kind.

Vetoes

Critics of divided government would do well to focus on the negative effects of veto politics, for this is one area where we can identify a clear impact of divided government. Not surprisingly, several studies show that over the course of our political history, use of the veto is related to opposition control of Congress.[24] With a somewhat finer measure, Rohde and Simon find that use of the veto in the post-World War II period goes up as the proportion of congressional seats controlled by the opposition party rises.[25] Still, as Ringelstein points out, the relationship is loose: Carter (unified government) and Nixon (divided) averaged exactly the same number of vetoes per year, and Eisenhower vetoed exactly as many bills (twenty-one) in 1953–54 when he had a Republican Congress as he vetoed in 1955–56 when Congress was Democratic.[26]

Such recent counterexamples notwithstanding, here is finally some impact of divided government. Whether out of genuine commitment to their party program, or the cynical desire to create electoral issues, congressional majorities push their disagreements with opposition presidents to the point that vetoes result.

A Further Objection

Let us stipulate that the foregoing negative findings regarding the effects of divided government are valid: divided governments are as legislatively productive as unified governments, and legislatures con-

[24]Jong R. Lee, "Presidential Vetoes from Washington to Nixon," *Journal of Politics* 37 (1975): 522–46; Gary Copeland, "When Congress and the President Collide: Why Presidents Veto Legislation," *Journal of Politics* 45 (1983): 696–710.

[25]David W. Rohde and Dennis M. Simon, "Presidential Vetoes and Congressional Response: A Study of Institutional Conflict," *American Journal of Political Science* 29 (1985): 397–427.

[26]Albert C. Ringelstein, "Presidential Vetoes: Motivations and Classification," in Harry A. Bailey, Jr., and Jay M. Shafritz. eds., *The American Presidency* (Chicago: Dorsey Press, 1988), 181.

trolled by the opposite party do not investigate the executive or reject the president's nominees more than legislatures controlled by the same party. Even so, critics of divided government might argue that governing under divided conditions is more difficult—more contentious; more consumptive of time, energy and other resources; and generally more costly psychically and materially—for all concerned.[27] That divided governments accomplish as much as unified governments might only indicate that officials work harder under such conditions; that investigations are no more frequent under divided conditions might only indicate that the executive works harder to foresee and preempt such investigations; that presidential nominations are about as successful under divided conditions might only indicate that presidents anticipate congressional objections and tailor their appointments accordingly. Certainly, arguments like these are plausible, even if difficult to verify. But such second-order effects are hardly the major consequences of divided government that are asserted by some of its critics.

Furthermore, even if true, such "anticipated reactions" arguments do not provide unqualified support for the critics of divided government. If divided government were to make governing more difficult and costly, that obviously would be a negative entry in the ledger, but certainly there are positive entries that should be weighed before a balanced judgment can be offered. Full scrutiny of presidential nominations and foreign policy proposals is one such positive entry; a more open policy process is another.

Breaking Up Those Iron Triangles

Discussions of American policy-making in the 1960s placed great importance on the notion of "subgovernments," more colloquially known as "iron triangles" or "cozy little triangles."[28] The vertices of

[27]In a study of hearings by the foreign relations committees of Congress, Peterson and Greene found that more questions were directed at executive branch witnesses when the committee was under the control of the opposing party. Paul E. Peterson and Jay P. Greene, "Partisanship and Consensus in the Making of Foreign Policy," unpublished manuscript.

[28]Douglas Cater, *Power in Washington* (New York: Random House, 1964); Ernest Griffith, *Congress: Its Contemporary Role* (New York: University Press, 1961).

the triangle were composed of a congressional committee, an executive agency, and an interest group constituency, which together determined public policy in an area under the specific jurisdiction of the committee and agency. According to the "how a bill becomes a law" accounts in civics books, national policy-making was the result of a majoritarian process, but according to the subgovernment model, national policy-making was often the product of unrepresentative minorities quietly adopting and overseeing self-interested policies in areas of special interest to them.

Certainly subgovernment decision-making continues to exist, and a few prominent examples can still be found, but most contemporary students of American national policy-making find the notion much less applicable today than it was a generation ago.[29] Some speak of subgovernments as having given way to more loosely organized "policy networks," while others simply find the concept of diminishing relevance.[30] Still others observe that, at a minimum, we must speak of iron rectangles to take account of the vastly increased role of the courts in policy-making.[31]

There are a number of plausible explanations for the declining importance of subgovernments in American politics. A greatly expanded universe of interest groups has made the environment of iron triangles much more conflictual: with so many groups (including "public interest" groups) ready to sound the alarms, there is less likelihood that small groups of like-minded conspirators can quietly

---

[29]While Randall Ripley and Grace Franklin continue to base their excellent discussion of national policy-making on the subgovernment model, their successive editions recognize the declining importance of subgovernments as traditionally conceived. For example, the fourth edition of *Congress, the Bureaucracy, and Public Policy* (Chicago: Dorsey Press, 1987) contains qualifications on pages 7–8 that were not present in the first edition.

[30]On networks see Hugh Heclo, "Issue Networks and the Executive Establishment," in Anthony King, ed., *The New American Political System* (Washington, DC: Brookings, 1978): 87–124. On the declining relevance of subgovernments, see Jeffrey Berry, "Subgovernments, Issue Networks, and Political Conflict," in Richard Harris and Sidney Milkis, eds., *Remaking American Politics* (Boulder, CO: Westview Press 1989), 239–260.

[31]James Q. Wilson, "The Politics of Regulation," in James Q. Wilson, ed., *The Politics of Regulation* (New York: Basic Books, 1980), passim.

adopt self-serving policies.[32] Similarly, the more active and adversarial media lessen the likelihood that subgovernment excesses can escape the glare of public attention. Still a third reason for the declining importance of subgovernments could be the much maligned rise of divided government.

When Richard Nixon appointed Howard Phillips to be the acting director of the Office of Economic Opportunity (OEO), Phillips boasted that he would consider his tenure a success if he were able to "dismantle" OEO.[33] This was hardly the kind of talk one would expect from a member in good standing of a "cozy little triangle," and Democratic members of Congress howled in protest. Ronald Reagan appointed Anne Gorsuch to administer the Environmental Protection Agency (EPA). Gorsuch promptly cut her budget and staff and relaxed federal pollution standards. Rather than cooperate with her, interest groups and Congress forced her resignation.

Evidently, the sentiments expressed and actions taken by these Nixon and Reagan appointees are not conducive to the smooth functioning of subgovernments. An implicit premise of the subgovernment model is nonpartisanship. Either the involved issue transcends partisanship (building dams, subsidizing shipping, and so forth) *and/or* one party dominates the governmental vertices of the triangle—the congressional committees and the executive agencies. When legislators and agency heads share common partisan bonds, the prospects for mutually advantageous alliances are enhanced; conversely, when divided government pits executive appointees of a Republican president against Democratic congressional committees, the prospects for conflict are enhanced.

In retrospect the subgovernment notion seems to have been most applicable to the era of unified government, especially the New Deal years.[34] This was a period in which a Democratic president appointed Democratic administrators who worked with Democratic committee

---

[32]Thomas Gais, Mark Peterson, and Jack Walker, "Interest Groups, Iron Triangles and Representative Institutions in American National Government," *British Journal of Political Science* 14 (1984): 161–85.

[33]"Senate Liberals Try to Save Community Action," *Congressional Quarterly Weekly Report* (3 March 1973): 431.

[34]A classic work on the subject details the operation of the Bureau of Indian Affairs during the New Deal era. See J. Leiper Freeman, *The Political Process: Executive Bureau-Legislative Committee Relations* (New York: Random House, 1965).

chairs, all of whom were overseen (in the most minimal sense) by Democratic judges.[35] With everything in the family, so to speak, subgovernments thrived. Democratic congressional committees had little incentive to investigate Democratic agencies. As for the Republicans, with no institutional base that would enable them to lick their adversaries, their best option was to join them, when they could.[36]

Moreover, consider the greatly expanded role of the courts in contemporary policy-making. In the unified government-subgovernment era, statutes could contain the most general and vague language because elected officials could trust political allies in the bureaucracy and judiciary to take care of the details. But when Republican bureaucrats publicly threaten to destroy Democratic programs, Democratic Congresses must be careful to spell out exactly what they mean. They may also increase the opportunities for judicial review of agency decisions in order to place additional constraints on agency actions. Thus, the courts increasingly are drawn into the fray as arbiters between the partisan opponents.[37]

Conflict? Yes, divided government probably does make executive-legislative relations more conflictual. But if the conflict serves to insure that public policies are more openly considered and more reflective of majoritarian sentiments, that conflict has a positive side. Is it so clear that we should prefer the quiet, non-conflictual, special interest policy-making of subgovernments?

Summary

As yet there is only a limited amount of systematic research on the effects of divided government. What there is, however, fails to sup-

---

[35]On the noninterventionist position of federal judges during the New Deal period see Martin Shapiro, "The Supreme Court's 'Return' to Economic Regulation," in Karen Orren and Stephen Skowronek, eds., *Studies in American Political Development*, Vol. 1 (New Haven, CT: Yale University Press, 1986), 91–141

[36]As a congressman, David Stockman complained bitterly about Republican support for Great Society programs after the money began to flow. "The Social Pork Barrel," *Public Interest* 39 (1975): 3–30.

[37]Of major significance, however, is that as of mid-1991 Reagan and Bush had appointed two-thirds of the members of the federal district courts. Thus, in the future we may see congressional Democrats attempt to limit the role of the courts in the administrative sphere.

port the stronger claims of the critics of divided government. Some divided governments are legislatively active, some are legislatively passive, and the relative proportions do not differ appreciably from the proportions of active and passive unified governments. Despite the budgetary difficulties of the 1980s, divided governments evidently do not have a monopoly on such difficulties. There is little evidence that divided government makes it more difficult for presidents to have their appointments and treaties approved, but even if it does, is this necessarily bad? Surely more intense scrutiny has some positive consequences that must be taken into consideration. Divided government may and probably does exacerbate the level of conflict among congressional committees, executive agencies, and the courts. But is this necessarily bad? Political scientists were highly critical of the "cozy little triangles" that flourished in the era of unified government. Divided government may and probably does encourage Congress and the president to play electoral games with the veto rather than compromise at some earlier stage, or decline to act at all. But is this necessarily bad? Perhaps the fact that government is divided in the first place reveals the lack of consensus on the policy.

All in all, the research surveyed above fits well with the general conclusion of David Rohde's exhaustive study of congressional support for presidents from Eisenhower to Reagan:

> Many analysts have decried the persistence of divided government in recent decades, arguing that it has undermined the federal government's ability to deal with national problems, leading to bitter conflict and policy stalemate. The results presented here indicate that such results are neither theoretically automatic, nor empirically inevitable.[38]

Divided Government and Electoral Accountability

In 1980 I wrote an essay entitled "The Decline of Collective Responsibility in American Politics."[39] Writing in an era that exalted popular participation and reacting to the sorry performance of the Carter administration—our last episode of unified government—I updated

---

[38]David W Rohde, "Divided Government, Agenda Change and Variations in Presidential Support in the House," paper presented at the Conference in Honor of William F. Riker, University of Rochester, October 1990, p. 31.
[39]*Daedalus* (Summer, 1980): 25–45.

the traditional arguments about the importance of party responsibility in American politics. With the weakening of party affiliations in the electorate and the decline of party organization as a force in campaigns, the inability of party to enforce cohesion in government inevitably had followed. Members of Congress were reelected on the basis of their individual records and would run no risks to aid a president of their party whose fate would have little or no bearing on theirs. The result was (among other things) an erosion of electoral accountability. Presidents were held accountable for the state of the economy and other aspects of the larger national well-being, but members of Congress could generally escape responsibility for the big picture by running on their personal relationships with their districts and their records of particularistic achievements. After all, no one could plausibly charge that one representative of 435 or one senator of 100 personally was responsible for stagflation or gas lines or budget deficits. An impersonal entity called "Congress" shared that responsibility with the president. But unlike the president, the collective "Congress" never appeared on the ballot. Thus, the president had come to bear greater political responsibility than his authority justified, while members of Congress had come to bear less than their responsibilities obligated. The point was not that party responsibility was the ideal, but that the alternative was irresponsibility, not some other form of responsibility. Thus, any reforms or developments that encouraged voters to support the party, not the person, were worth considering and encouraging.

That was 15 years ago, and if responsibility was problematic in American politics even when government was unified, the problem is compounded when government is divided. Presidents blame Congress for obstructing carefully crafted solutions, while members of Congress attack the president for lack of leadership. Citizens genuinely cannot tell who is to blame, and the meaning of election outcomes becomes increasingly confused.

The reluctance of Americans to impose collective responsibility on their leaders often gives our politics a comical tone. During the 1988 election campaign, there was a great to-do about George Bush's role in the Iran-Contra affair. How much did he know? How responsible was he? Some elements of the media became obsessed with these questions. Bush was able to turn that obsession to his advantage in the celebrated live encounter with Dan Rather. European observers must have viewed the entire episode as pure silliness. Was Bush responsible? Of course he was. He was a member of the administration in power and he did not resign in protest; therefore, he was responsible—100 percent. The voter cannot mark her ballot Reagan 75 percent guilty, Bush 50 percent guilty, Shultz 35 percent, Weinberger 20 percent; she can mark only for or against. The only way to give office-holders the proper incentives is to hold *all* of them *fully* responsible for the decisions with which they are associated. Nothing else will suffice. In contrasting his vice-presidential choice to that of Bush, Dukakis argued that if a scheme such as Iran-Contra were hatched when Lloyd Bentsen was in the room, the upright Bentsen—unlike Bush—would quickly squelch such madness. Maybe so, but as Madison cautioned long ago, we should not depend on the personal uprightness of our leaders. The best insurance against a future occurrence such as the Iran-Contra affair would have been the destruction of Bush's political career, and Republican losses of ten Senate and forty House seats. Then, we could be relatively confident that when some future scheme was hatched, someone in the room would ask "Do you remember what happened in 1988?"[40]

Although collective responsibility is a blunt instrument, it is the only one we have. In obscuring responsibility for government actions and the results thereof, divided control exacerbates the already serious problems of responsibility that are inherent in American politics. On this matter I am in substantial agreement with Sundquist. But as always, there is another side to the argument. When we are talking about much of economic and social policy and mundane matters of foreign policy, the accountability argument is compelling.

But there are policies that have different, sometimes irreversible, effects. A unified Republican government under Reagan would

---

[40]At this point one will hear the standard objection: what if the Republicans *had* accepted full responsibility and the voters chose *not* to punish them at the polls? We must be prepared to live with such outcomes. Except in clear, deliberate, and serious violations of the law, the ultimate locus of responsibility in a democracy must be electoral, not legal. In this lawyer-dominated society such a position may seem heretical, but see L. H. LaRue, *Political Discourse: A Case Study of the Watergate Affair* (Athens: University of Georgia Press, 1988).

have offered the electorate a clear choice in 1984 and 1988. In the abstract that would be desirable, but one suspects that the relatives of dead Nicaraguans would take small consolation in the knowledge that Americans had a clear choice in 1984 and 1988. Theoretically, a self-confident unified government could follow a policy path that would kill many of its constituents before it ever was held to account at the next election, as in the case of Viet Nam, where Americans died throughout 1967 and 1968 while waiting for an opportunity to pass on the administration's policy. Divided government may limit the potential for a society to gain through government actions, but it may similarly limit the potential for a society to lose because of government actions. Cutler and Sundquist may regret the opportunities foregone; their critics may appreciate the pitfalls avoided. Both points of view are valid, and which one ultimately prevails is the decision of the electorate.

The irony, of course, is that divided government may make it more difficult for the electorate to make such decisions. Knowing that voters find it difficult to assess responsibility, both president and Congress find an added incentive to posture and procrastinate, which in turn may lead to steadily deteriorating conditions. Lives are destroyed very quickly in wars, but they can also be destroyed more slowly and less dramatically when government fails to deal with challenges arising from the social and economic worlds. The evidence reviewed earlier in this chapter suggests that divided governments and unified governments as yet have not differed significantly in their capacity to meet challenges. Given contemporary conditions—a persistent state of divided government—we must hope that such initial findings are borne out by future developments.

C H A P T E R 7

COMPARATIVE PERSPECTIVE

If we look beyond Washington, however, we can see that unified government is not an anachronism in modern democratic society. It exists in most of the other industrial democracies.—Lloyd Cutler.[1]

As a political science professor, I am professionally delighted to note that such an erroneous claim was made by a lawyer and published by a respected law review. Most of the world's governments are *not* unified governments like the idealized British parliamentary system or the unified American system of the first half of the twentieth century. Rather, governments controlled jointly by coalitions of two or more parties are, of course, the norm in the European democracies, and in democracies generally. Germany is governed by a coalition of Christian Democrats and Free Democrats, while France is governed by a coalition of socialist parties. For most of the 1980s Italy was governed by a "pentapartito"—a five-party coalition. The list can easily be extended.[2] The relevance of these examples for our discussion is apparent. Cutler's colleague Sundquist refers to the American condition of divided government as coalition government.[3] Conversely, Laver and Shepsle observe that the commonly observed minority governments are, in a sense, divided govern-

---

[1]Lloyd N. Cutler, "Now Is the Time for All Good Men," *William and Mary Law Review* 30 (1989): 399.

[2]Moreover, it seems a safe bet that the newly emerging democracies of Central and Eastern Europe will adopt various forms of proportional representation likely to eventuate in multi-party coalition governments.

[3]James Sundquist, "Needed: A Political Theory for the New Era of Coalition Government in the United States," *Political Science Quarterly* 10 (1988): 613–35.

ments.[4] To the extent that coalition governments and divided governments are analogous, the rise of divided government in the United States makes us more like the rest of the world's democracies, not less.

The analogy between divided government and coalition government is worth exploring at some length. In multi-party parliamentary systems like those common in Europe, one party rarely wins a majority of seats in the parliament. Typically, two or more parties that together comprise a parliamentary majority must negotiate an agreement on a division of cabinet posts, including that of the prime minister—generally the chief executive.[5] Thus, in the typical unitary parliamentary system, parties in the government have partial control of the full power-of-government. In contrast, divided government in a separation-of-powers system like that of the United States gives each party full control of part of the power of government.[6] The contrast is real, but the larger similarity is important: in both cases each party needs the acquiescence of others in order to govern. In both European coalition governments and American divided governments, one party cannot govern alone.

The preceding insight has an array of consequences. Most generally, the analogy between divided government and coalition government suggests that much of our theoretical treatment of two-party and multi-party politics exaggerates the differences.

Two-Party *versus* Multi-Party Electoral Competition

Some three decades ago, Anthony Downs published *An Economic Theory of Democracy*, the cornerstone of the modern theory of elections.[7] Downs drew a sharp distinction between two-party and

---

[4]Michael Laver and Kenneth A. Shepsle, "Divided Government: America Is Not 'Exceptional,' " *Governance* 4 (1991): 250–69.

[5]In Fifth Republic France there is a separately elected president, in addition to a prime minister supported by a majority of parliament.

[6]Obvious practical questions like party cohesion arise here, but similar questions arise in the case of coalition governments as well.

[7]New York: Harper and Row, 1957.

multi-party systems, concluding that they would show different patterns of party behavior, voter behavior, and policy outcomes. Whether or not as a direct consequence of Downs's argument, the theories of two-party and multi-party democracy have since developed relatively independently of one another.[8] Two-party theory emphasizes electoral competition, examining the strategies of parties and the reactions of voters.[9] In contrast, multi-party theory focuses heavily on government formation, asking how parties would coalesce once the votes were counted and seats in parliament assigned.[10] For some time the intersection of these two enterprises was minimal, but in recent years new points of contact have developed as a younger generation of scholars has extended the reach of existing theory.[11]

This theoretical convergence is welcome because in all likelihood the original Downsian distinction between two-party and multi-party systems was greatly overdrawn. The contemporary American experience with divided government forms the basis for that claim. Working with an implicit assumption that unified government is the norm, we have failed to appreciate the theoretical similarities of apparently differing phenomena like divided control and coalition government. Upon reflection, behavior thought to be different may be similarly motivated—splitting a ticket and supporting a third party, for example. In addition, policy outcomes in the

---

[8]Downs's arguments probably made some contribution to this separate development, but undoubtedly an American scholarly community found two-party competition to be the more natural starting point for a theory of elections.

[9]Taking their inspiration from noncooperative game theory, analysts such as Otto Davis, Melvin Hinich, Peter Ordeshook, John Ledyard, Gerald Kramer, Richard McKelvey, and Norman Schofield successively elaborated the Downsian spatial model into an impressive theoretical edifice. For a survey of this body of work, see James Enelow and Melvin Hinich, *The Spatial Theory of Voting* (Cambridge, England: Cambridge University Press, 1984).

[10]Taking their inspiration largely from cooperative game theory, William Riker, Michael Leiserson, Robert Axelrod, Michael Laver, and Norman Schofield advanced differing theories about how government coalitions would form. For a survey see Michael Laver and Norman Schofield, *Multiparty Government* (Oxford, England: Oxford University Press, 1990).

[11]David Austin-Smith and Jeffrey Banks, "Elections, Coalitions, and Legislative Outcomes," *American Political Science Review* 82 (1988): 405–22.

two kinds of systems may be more similar than sometimes asserted. After first reviewing the Downsian arguments, I will discuss some implications of the contemporary American experience for our notions of electoral competition.

Party Systems According to Downs

Downs viewed politics in multi-party systems as much more complex than politics in two-party systems, so much so that he considered political rationality in multi-party systems to be somewhat problematic—his principal chapter on the subject is titled "Problems of Rationality Under Coalition Governments." Among other things, Downs's analysis led him to conclude the following:[12]

1. Though rational voting is more important in multiparty systems than in two-party systems, it is more difficult and less effective.
2. In systems normally governed by coalitions, voters are under pressure to behave irrationally.
3. Party ideologies and policies in multiparty systems are more sharply defined than in two-party systems, but actual government programs are less integrated in the former than in the latter.

Cutler and Sundquist probably would agree with these general claims, at least the first two, but contemporary experience suggests that each proposition is questionable.

Downs saw the voters' problem as particularly acute in multiparty systems.[13] In a section entitled "The Complexity and Difficulty of Being Rational," he observed that "each vote helps elect at

---

[12]Downs, *An Economic Theory*, 143.

[13]In Downs's stylized multi-party system, voters cast a single vote for a party. Seats are allocated according to strict proportional representation within a single national district (ibid., 144). Throughout the analysis he assumes that no party wins a majority of seats.

most only part of a government." Moreover, "each vote supports a party which will have to compromise its policies even if elected; hence the policies of this party are not the ones which a vote for it actually supports." Consequently, for a voter to behave in truly rational fashion, she must estimate the outcome of the parties' bargaining, which entails estimating how many seats each will win, which in turn entails estimating how all other voters are likely to behave.[14] Given the information and computational capacity required to make such (interdependent) calculations (not to mention the miniscule value of any single individual vote—an argument that comes later), we cannot expect voters to make such calculations. Instead, the complexity of the task they face leads many voters to act irrationally, to "treat elections as preference polls" rather than as mechanisms for selecting governments.[15]

I do not contest Downs's description of the difficulties multi-party coalition systems pose for rational voting. What I do question is his assumption that two-party systems are intrinsically less demanding. The two-party system that forms the basis of Downs's earlier analysis is one in which "At each election, the party which receives the most votes...controls the entire government until the next election."[16] The party winning full control is "a team of men seeking to control the governing apparatus.... By *team*, we mean a coalition whose members agree on all their goals instead of on just part of them."[17] Apparently, Downs has abstracted a British government of mid-century; his stylized two-party system is one with a unitary form and two cohesive parties that alternate in office. Clearly, however, with its cohesive parties and centralized institutions, the British system was the exceptional two-party system, not the norm. Unitary Britain is one extreme case, and federal, separation-of-powers America is the other. The rest of the world's two-party systems are arrayed in between, albeit most are closer to the British pole than to the American. But divided government is a real possibil-

[14]Ibid., 146–47.
[15]Ibid., 143.
[16]Ibid., 11.
[17]Ibid., 25.

ity in Fifth Republic France, as well as in several other democracies. And in such systems it is a possibility that sometimes comes to pass.[18]

Divided Government as Coalition Government

James Sundquist has decried the "new era of coalition government" in the United States. His use of the familiar European term is appropriate. In the stylized multi-party system, power is concentrated in the hands of a single institution called the "cabinet," which is supported by a majority in the parliament. Generally no party receives a majority, so a coalition of parties must form to select and maintain the executive. Each party wins partial control of the full power of government. In contrast, in a two-party system characterized by separation of powers and independent elections, one party wins control of each institution of government (assuming tie-breaking mechanisms), but the same party may not win all the institutions. Thus, each party wins full control of part of the power of government. In both systems, parties may have to share control of government power, though we express that sharing in terms of ministries in the one case and in terms of branches of government in the other. In either case policies cannot be adopted unless the parties can compromise their differences and agree upon a course of action. Scholars may choose to call an agreement in one context a "coalition" and an agreement in another context a "compromise," "deal," or "bargain," but such terminological differences should not obscure the theoretical similarity of the agreements.

Figure 7-1A depicts three-party competition in a two-dimensional policy space. The conservative party (C) is conservative on both economic and social (lifestyle, environment) issues, the "old" liberal party (L) is liberal on economic issues but less so on lifestyle issues, and the new politics party (N) is quite liberal on both issues. Assuming that any two of the three parties constitute a majority, the

---

[18]For purposes of this presentation, I am ignoring divisions of party control across federal levels. That complication means that divided control can occur even in systems that are unitary at the highest level—Canada's, for example.

standard analysis concludes that the outcome of the coalition bargain will lie somewhere on the contract curves between pairs of parties—the line segments connecting them.[19] Now consider Figure 7-1B, where the axes are interchanged and the parties are relabelled "President Reagan" (P), "Republican Senate" (S), and "Democratic House" (H). The details of the bargaining depicted in Figure 7-1B differ from those in Figure 7-1A—only in the special and unusual case of two-thirds majorities in both Houses do any two of the institutions in Figure 7-1B constitute a majority—but the general point is the same. Any policy adopted must lie on the contract "curve" of the three institutions, which is the triangle in this case.[20] Both figures illustrate a situation in which parties must bargain and negotiate to form a "coalition" capable of acting. And in both situations *Downsian rational voters must anticipate the possible coalitions and the policies they will produce.* Thus, rational voters in the two-party case may not have an easier task than those in the multi-party case. In fact, some considerations make their task more difficult. For example, coalitions in the multi-party case typically extend across time and issues, but bargains in the two-party case generally are issue specific. Thus, the rational voter in the two-party case must anticipate the decisive coalition on each issue, whereas her counterpart in the multi-party case needs to make only one overall calculation. (I do not for a moment argue that people actually do this, only that a consistent extension of the Downsian model to divided governments requires that they do.)

On the other hand, the task facing the voter in the two-party case is easier in that the voter can indicate an explicit preference for the coalition she prefers, and thereby send a clearer signal to the government. That is, in an American presidential election the rational voter

[19]Laver and Shepsle have recently pointed out that such an analysis ignores the existence of a status quo and features of the government formation process that may alter this simple conclusion. Their point is well taken when the question is one of modelling the coalition process, but my point here is just to indicate the qualitative similarities of government formation in two- and multi-party systems. Michael Laver and Kenneth Shepsle, "Coalitions and Cabinet Government," *American Political Science Review* 84 (1990): 873–90.

[20]For just such a representation of policy formation in American environmental policy-making, see Mathew McCubbins, Roger Noll, and Barry Weingast, "Structure and Process, Politics and Policy," *Virginia Law Review* 75 (1989): 431–82.

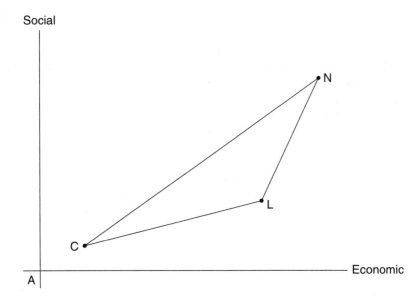

Figure 7-1 (A) Three-Party Bargaining Situation

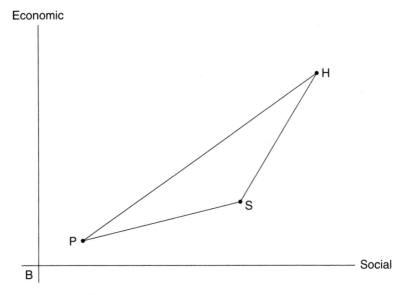

Figure 7-1 (B) Three-Institution Bargaining Situation

118

must consider the likely policy product of eight possible institutional alignments:

1. Democratic president, Senate, House
2. Democratic president and House, Republican Senate
3. Democratic president and Senate, Republican House
4. Democratic president, Republican Senate and House
5. Republican president, Democratic Senate and House
6. Republican president and Senate, Democratic House
7. Republican president and House, Democratic Senate
8. Republican president, Senate, House

Interestingly, these eight governmental forms are exactly the same number of *alternative coalitions* that may form in a three-party unitary system.[21] But the American voter has more choices (eight) than the voter endowed with one vote in a three-party parliamentary system (three). Generations of scholars have noted that voters in multi-party systems enjoy a wider array of choices than voters in two-party systems, but commonplace though it may be, the observation is incorrect unless buttressed with assumptions about greater policy differences among the parties in the multi-party system. For in a two-party system with a separation-of-powers, voters often have *numerically* more choices than they have in a multi-party system—only with nine or more parties would they have more choices than they have in the present American system. Furthermore, whereas the complexity of the calculations in the multi-party system encourages voters to resort to using their vote as an expression of party preference rather than a means for selecting a government, the option of splitting their ticket in a separation-of-powers system enables voters *to vote directly for the coalition they most prefer*—thus eliminating some of the disparity between

---

[21]The grand coalition, three two-party coalitions, three one-party minority governments, and the null coalition. Empirically, minority governments are more common than is often supposed. The null coalition might represent a breakdown of negotiations. On minority governments, see Kaare Strom, "Party Goals and Government Performance in Parliamentary Democracies," *American Political Science Review* 79 (1985): 738–54.

expressing a preference and contributing to the selection of a government.

All in all, it would seem that if the complexities of voting in multi-party systems threaten to overwhelm voters, then one must *ipso facto* conclude much the same about the complexities of voting in two-party systems. that permit divided government. We can adduce arguments on either side of the question, as illustrated above, but the argument for significantly greater complexity in the multi-party case appears to be considerably exaggerated.

Ticket-Splitting or Third Parties?

In the Downsian analysis, voters in two-party systems face a simple decision of casting their single vote for one of two parties that, for reputational reasons, will act in accord with its previous performance and/or promises if elected.[22] Matters clearly are not so simple in separation-of-powers systems with independent elections. Voters have one vote for each office and are free to choose different parties as they move down the ballot.

As we have noted, most discussions of split-ticket voting in the United States treat it as a by-product of other forces rather than as an instance of rational behavior. But if ticket-splitting has any purposive basis, as discussed in Chapter 5, an interesting analogy between split-ticket voting and third-party voting arises.

Consider the conditions under which third parties decide to enter or exit the electoral arena. One situation in which a third party may enter is when the two existing parties are almost identical ("there's not a dime's worth of difference"). A third party might then emerge to represent a point of view ignored by the existing parties. A second situation in which a third party might emerge is when the existing parties are polarized, so that centrist voters are denied a centrist choice. In the second situation, the ability to split a ticket may undercut the motive to support a third, centrist, party, since the electorate can impose a compromise outcome even where the established parties are determined to avoid one.

[22]Downs, *An Economic Theory*, 103–9.

Thus, in decentralized two-party systems, ticket-splitters may play a role similar to that of minor party supporters in more centralized two-party systems. In each case their behavior may reflect an unwillingness to accept the choices offered by the dominant parties. Which outlet they choose will be partially determined by the system's electoral institutions: *ceteris paribus*, the more friendly they are to ticket-splitting, the less friendly they are to third parties.[23] Once again, our profession might caution that institutional reforms can have unintended and counterproductive consequences. Lloyd Cutler has proposed a unified ballot for president, vice president, senator, and representative as a cure for the contemporary divisions in American government.[24] Ironically, if the preceding analysis has any validity, then adoption of a proposal like Cutler's would lead to increased support for minor parties. Consider that in Britain, where voters have no opportunity to split, the Liberal/SDP Alliance gained strength after the Labour party lurched to the left, and declined from its 1980s high point after Labour moved back toward the center. It should not be too surprising that in democracies, majorities find ways to avoid having minority programs shoved down their throats.

Ideological Clarity and Policy Coherence

Based on his spatial analysis, Downs concludes that the centrist tendency of two-party competition will lead parties to adopt similar policies and to "becloud their policies in a fog of ambiguity."[25] In contrast, the exigencies of multi-party competition will lead parties to take clear and distinct stands. In this conclusion Downs was simply reaffirming conventional wisdom. Somewhat more original was the observation that the process of coalition formation in multiparty systems would turn clear and distinct electoral stands into incoherent government programs, whereas the unclear and indistinct elec-

---

[23]This argument applies only to the case of two polarized parties. Where the parties are nearly identical, supporting a third party is the only option for the voter unhappy with a pure party option.

[24]Lloyd Cutler, "To Form a Government," *Foreign Affairs* (Fall 1980): 126–43.

[25]Downs, *An Economic Theory,* 136.

toral stands of two-party systems would eventuate in coherent government policies.[26] Upon reflection, the case for both conclusions is weak.

As for the conventional wisdom about the "me-too," "middle-of-the-road" quality of two-party competition, the empirical technology for cross-national comparisons does not exist. On a more impressionistic level, however, I have been surprised in recent years to hear European visitors opine that they saw at least as much distance between the Reagan Republicans and Mondale Democrats in the 1980s as the distance between the principal parties in France and Italy. Ditto for the Thatcher Conservatives and Labour. Whether such impressions of relative distance are correct or not, the absence of party activists and other manifestations of internal party politics from the Downsian model and its progeny clearly undermine theoretical conclusions about the centrist tendencies of two-party competition.[27] It is generally recognized that the two American parties are further apart today than they were a generation ago, and internal party politics is widely viewed as a major part of the explanation.[28]

I am more interested in the second conclusion—that two-party systems produce more coherent policies than multi-party systems, because this proposition also seems to be undermined by the existence of divided government. In either type of system, two possibilities are open after the election. First, a stalemate may ensue. In a multi-party system, the parties may be unable to form a coalition, or once formed, they may not be able to agree upon a program. In a two-party system, the parties controlling different institutions may

---

[26]"Proposition 4: In a multi-party system governed by a coalition, the government takes less effective action to solve basic social problems, and its policies are less integrated and consistent, than in a two-party system." Ibid., 297.

[27]There have been some attempts to take internal party politics into account, but these have occupied a tangential status in the research program. See John Aldrich, "A Downsian Spatial Model with Party Activism," *American Political Science Review* 77 (1983): 974–90.

[28]Jeane Kirkpatrick, *The New Presidential Elite: Men and Women in National Politics* (New York: Russell Sage, 1976); Warren E. Miller and M. Kent Jennings, *Parties in Transition: A Longitudinal Study of Party Elites and Party Supporters* (New York: Russell Sage, 1986); William Crotty and John S. Jackson, III, *Presidential Primaries and Nominations* (Washington, DC: CQ Press, 1985).

be unable to agree upon appointments and policies. Much more likely—in either type of system—the parties compromise and government continues to produce and implement public policies. Compromise can take either of two ideal-typical forms.

In one form the parties compromise on each issue, leading to some moderate or centrist outcome (relative to the conflicting parties' ideals). Given this form of compromise, there is no logical reason for policy to be incoherent—*in either two-party or multi-party systems*. Policies will represent some middle ground between parties A, B, and C in the coalition government, or a middle ground between party A in control of the presidency and party B in control of the Congress in a divided government. Moderate policies may not please ideologues, and may be attacked as "mushy," but there is no particular reason for them to be incoherent. *Coherence* is not synonymous with *extremity*.

If compromise occurs not on each issue, but across issues, so that one party controls issue X and another issue Y, where issues X and Y are relatively dearer to the collective hearts of parties A and B, then we do not get a coherent, if centrist, government program, but rather, an incoherent one in which government policy is (say) liberal on issue X, centrist on Y, and conservative on Z. But what does two-party or multi-party competition have to do with this conclusion? In a coalition government, party A might be content with control over the defense ministry, party B with control over the finance ministry, and party C with control over the labor and social services ministry. The result is incoherence. In divided government the president and Congress might reach an implicit understanding that gives the president higher defense spending and lower taxes, while the Congress gets increases in domestic spending. The result, according to McCubbins, is deficits and what many would see as incoherence.[29] But the *form of the compromise* is what produces the incoherence, not the number of parties involved in it. Unless research shows that coalition governments generally compromise by trading off control

[29]Mathew McCubbins, "Party Governance and U.S. Budget Deficits: Divided Government and Fiscal Stalemate," in Alberto Alesina and Geoffrey Carliner, eds., *Politics and Economics in the 1980s* (Chicago: University of Chicago Press, 1991), 83–111.

over issues, whereas two-party divided governments generally compromise by choosing moderate positions on each issue, the Downsian conclusion fails.[30] Coalition governments are not intrinsically
more likely to produce incoherent policies. Leaving Downs to one
side, if two-party divided governments do generally compromise
by choosing moderate positions on each issue, then the Cutler-
Sundquist conclusion falls as well: divided governments are not
intrinsically more likely to produce incoherent policies than are unified governments. We can cite selected examples on either side, but
so far as I know, the general form that compromise takes in different
systems is an open question.

Summary

Divided government in two-party systems undercuts the longstand-
ing theoretical divide between the analysis of two-party systems and
the more common multi-party systems. In the first place, divided
government calls into serious question the abstract theoretical char-
acterization of two-party systems. In the second place, taking
divided government as a type of coalition government shows that
features of the two systems thought to be unique actually may be different empirical manifestations of a common impulse—split-ticket
voting and voting for third parties is the example discussed. Finally,
standard generalizations about the kinds of policies generated by
two-party and multi-party political systems are undercut by the
existence of divided government in two-party systems. Far from the
rise of divided government's making the United States even more
"exceptional" among the world's democracies, the rise of divided
government may well make our politics more similar.

---

[30]Of course, there is another, independent, argument that single-member districts
encourage particularized (read "incoherent") policy-making. While single-member
districts are common in two-party systems, the critical variable appears to be the
opportunity for legislators to construct a "personal vote," since multi-party systems
with preference voting also show tendencies to particularize. Bruce Cain, John
Ferejohn, and Morris Fiorina, *The Personal Vote* (Cambridge, MA: Harvard University
Press, 1987)

CHAPTER 8

THE RESEARCH AGENDA

The leitmotif of Sundquist's important essay is the intellectual challenge divided government poses for political science. Sundquist maintains that American political science traditionally has accepted a version of the responsible party doctrine combined with a belief in the critical need for presidential leadership. Many of the major theorists of American political science—V. O. Key, Pendleton Herring, E. E. Schattschneider, and various others—lived their entire professional lives in the first half of the twentieth century, the unusual era of unified government (Table 2-1). Even the next generation lived their formative years during the latter days of that period. The result is that almost to this day our general accounts of the operation of American national government presuppose unified party control.[1]

While conceding the dangers in evaluating government operation in different eras, Sundquist contends that the American version of party government did function passably well, at least relative to the current period of divided government. But whether right or wrong, he expresses disappointment that most of his colleagues have not joined the issue, charging that political scientists evade

---

[1]Consider the ongoing controversy between "Congressional dominance" theorists of executive-legislative relations and the forceful critiques offered by substantive experts. I was puzzled by my inclination to agree with both sides until I realized the importance of divided government in this debate. The modellers worked from a textbook portrait that unfortunately is dated. Until quite recently the textbook portrait reflected the congressional studies of the 1960s and an even older executive branch literature, much of it developed by veterans of the New Deal and their students. These literatures implicitly presume that in the natural order of the universe a president appoints an agency head of his party who then deals with a congressional

125

what is surely one of the most crucial intellectual questions facing students of American government—one that the previous generation of political scientists explicitly asked and answered.... fence straddling on this issue is not intellectually defensible. Either the dominant pre-1954 view of the desirability of party government and presidential leadership as the model and the ideal was right or it was wrong. That two systems so diametrically opposite as party government and coalition could serve the country equally well is a virtual mathematical impossibility.... One or the other necessarily has to be the superior model for America, and political scientists have a responsibility to determine which it is and inform the country of their judgment.[2]

Most of us are willing enough to accept intellectual responsibility (though I doubt that the country waits with bated breath for the pronouncements of political science professors). The problem is that some of us do not see matters quite so clearly as Sundquist does. In my view an evaluation of the current state of divided government *must* be equivocal, and it must remain so until we fully understand the reasons that it has come about—why voters are splitting their tickets—as discussed in earlier chapters. For Sundquist, divided government is simply an accident: "the United States has its own unique version of coalition government—not a coalition voluntarily entered into by the parties but one forced upon them by the accidents of the electoral process."[3] Evidently regarding party decline and incum-

---

(continued)

committee chair of the same party. The critics, however, work from a background of two decades of divided government that provides examples of presidential appointees who boast that their success will be determined by the length of time it takes to destroy their programs and/or agencies (see Chapter 6). The next generation of models must recognize that under divided government the executive and the legislature have much less common ground than they have under unified control. Barry R. Weingast and Mark J. Moran, "Bureaucratic Discretion or Congressional Control? Regulatory Policymaking by the Federal Trade Commision," *Journal of Political Economy* 91 (1983): 765–800. Cf. Terry M. Moe, "An Assessment of the Positive Theory of 'Congressional Dominance,'" *Legislative Studies Quarterly* 12 (1987): 475–520; James Q. Wilson, *Bureaucracy: What Government Agencies Do and Why They Do It* (New York: Basic Books, 1989), chap. 13.
[2] Sundquist, 633–34.
[3] Ibid., 614.

bency as sufficient explanations of the present situation, Sundquist explicitly rejects purposeful explanations because they assume that

> divided government is the people's intent, more or less conscious, rather than the essentially chance outcome of the electoral system that was not designed by those who use it. Clearly the latter is the case: divided government is a historical and procedural accident.[4]

If divided government is only an accident, a by-product of a chaotic electoral system, Sundquist's indictment gains force. To the extent that we can explain ticket-splitting by what I have referred to as "accidental explanations," divided government with attendant losses in efficiency (though we have had trouble identifying them—recall Chapter 6) has few offsetting benefits. On the other hand, if what I have called "purposeful explanations" have any validity as explanations of ticket-splitting, Sundquist's case is undercut. Recall Schattschneider's dictum that "Democracy was made for the people, not the people for democracy."[5] If it can be shown that the ticket-splitting of a significant proportion of the citizenry reflects a lack of confidence in the elites of both parties, who are we to recommend that they make a clear choice? If Americans believe that Republican party elites like to shoot up small countries and Democratic party elites believe that America is the problem, not the solution, should they be forced to entrust the entire conduct of foreign policy to either party? If citizens believe that Republican elites wish to redistribute from poor to rich, while Democratic elites have never met a tax they didn't like, should they be forced to give either party unfettered control of economic affairs? If citizens think Republicans are tough on crime but dismiss acid rain as a figment of the liberal imagination, while Democrats are good on the environment but believe that there are no criminals, only oppressed victims of society, should citizens be forced to make a clear choice? Perhaps those worried about the future of American democracy should be more concerned with our leaders and less with our voters.

---

[4]Ibid., 633–34.
[5]E. E. Schattschneider, *The Semi-Sovereign People* (Hinsdale, IL: Dryden Press, 1975), 132.

What about race? Next to the economy, it is the most important single issue in American politics. In the spring of 1991, a battle had been raging in Washington over a civil rights bill designed to overturn a number of recent Supreme Court decisions. Led by President Bush, Republicans had labelled it a "quota bill," while Democrats counter that Republican tactics indicate at best the most cynical form of electoral politics, and at worst, outright racism. What is actually the case? I suspect that the American people see matters much like op-ed page columnists across the political spectrum:

> This bill is no longer about justice. There is too much in it, and there is not enough. The 1991 civil rights bill is about politics and constituencies and hiring lawyers to frame language that will damage your political opponent.
>
> It is about Republicans who feed on racial alienation, who fly toward any scent of racial polarization. And it is about Democrats who can't say no to the civil rights lobby.[6]

> Somewhere between the ridiculous (It's a quota bill) and the preposterous (President Bush is a racialist) lie the views of most Americans; they hate discrimination, are uncomfortable with any form of racial preference, and detest racial politics of all kinds.[7]

> The Bush argument reeks of racial divisions, a tape nobody wants to keep playing. The civil rights argument is stuck on a 30-year-old legal agenda. Most Americans argue ambidextrously. They acknowledge that prejudice still exists, that racism is alive *and* that rigid quotas go against another code of fairness.[8]

If these commentators have accurately captured the perspective of the American people, consider what unified government demands of them. They are to give full control of the national government either to a party whose activists and appointees have supported busing and racial quotas or to a party whose activists and appointees cynically stir the pot of racial animosity. If, instead, the citizenry chooses to split control of government so as to frustrate both parties,

[6]Steve Daley, "A Bill About Politics—Not Justice," *The Boston Globe* (4 June 1991): 15.
[7]Thomas Oliphant, "The Big Campaign Test: Politician vs. Disillusioned Voter," *The Boston Globe* (12 June 1991): 19.
[8]Ellen Goodman, "Civil Rights Outside the Beltway," *The Boston Globe* (13 June 1991): 19

should they be blamed? On the contrary, perhaps they should be praised for frustrating the arrogant, cynical, and self-serving elites who wish to govern them.

If further research on split-ticket voting in American elections concludes that divided government is no more than "a historical and procedural accident," then a responsible political science should respond to Sundquist's challenge. What are the costs of divided government? If they are significant, how can the system be made to work better, and how might we return to the more unified conditions of previous times? On the other hand, if further research on split-ticket voting concludes that purpose as well as caprice underlies such behavior, then a different sort of challenge arises. Over the past generation, what conditions have led the party system to develop in such a way that a critical minority of Americans believe that divided government, with its potential inefficiency and irresponsibility, is preferable to a unified government that would act more efficiently and responsibly but in the service of ends they do not accept?

If the preferences of the electorate should prove to be a significant factor underlying the current condition of divided government, then that condition should be seen as a legitimate outcome of our constitutional system, however much it may contrast with earlier historical experience or the preferences of some commentators. The Constitution sought to buttress "parchment barriers" by pitting ambition against ambition, and the principal means of doing that was to elect public officials at different times, by different people, and for somewhat different reasons. If Americans choose to divide institutional control among the contending parties, they are only availing themselves of an option explicitly provided in their founding charter. An invigorated separation of powers may be a nuisance in an era of activist government, but it certainly is not something alien to our traditions.

Thus, the immediate task is to renew our commitment to the study of the behavior of the American electorate, not only in presidential and House elections, but also in Senate elections and in American state elections. Ticket-splitting and other aspects of the relationships between voting for different offices should become a central focus of research, rather than a sideline. As always, political science owes society investigation before evaluation and recommendation.

THE 1992 AND 1994 ELECTIONS

The 1992 National Elections

For the media and for many popular commentators on American politics, the main story of the 1992 elections was a story of change. Bill Clinton broke the supposed Republican "lock" on the presidency, only the second time since 1964 that a Democrat had been able to poll more votes than a Republican at the presidential level. Certainly that was a noteworthy change from recent electoral history, and understandably it became the focus of a news establishment that defines news largely in terms of things that change.

To those who looked closely at the underlying reality, however, the story was as much a story of continuity as of change. Like his regional predecessor in 1976, Clinton's victory occurred under exceptional conditions.[1] Although his popular vote margin over Bush was a comfortable 5.6 percent and his electoral vote margin was overwhelming, the presence of Ross Perot in the race clouded the picture, denying Clinton a majority of the popular vote in all but one state, his home state of Arkansas. The most detailed analyses that have been done conclude that Perot took about as many votes from Clinton as from Bush, suggesting that Clinton's popular vote margin over Bush in a two-way race would have been about the same as Bush's 1988 margin over Michael Dukakis. But all in all, voters

---

[1] In 1976 Carter was running against the *appointed* vice president of a president who had resigned in disgrace, in the aftermath of a serious recession. Under such conditions it was less noteworthy that a Democrat won than that he won by such a narrow margin—less than one percent.

were relatively unenthusiastic about both major party candidates in 1992.[2]

Whatever the uncertainties and ambiguities, Clinton won, and, given that the Democratic lock on the Congress continued, unified government was restored to the national level. There had been much speculation in the media about 1992 being the "year of the outsider." Congress had been buffeted by a series of scandals—the Keating 5, the House Post Office, the House Bank, Rep. Danny Rostenkowski—and popular esteem for the institution was at historic lows. Approval of the performance of Congress, for instance, was below 20 percent, in contrast to more normal (albeit still low) levels of about 35 percent.[3] Disgust with the campaign finance system was widespread. Term-limit proposals passed wherever they were put on the ballot.

But despite such a generally negative view of Congress, constituents continued to view their own representatives and senators much more favorably than they viewed the collective Congress, although 1992 approval levels in the 50–60 percent range for individual members of Congress were lower than the 60–70 range that was normal in the 1970s and 1980s.[4] As a consequence of this continued differentiation between individuals and the collectivity, the year of the outsider was much less apparent than was feared by some Democrats and hoped for by some Republicans. In the House, many of the more tainted incumbents either retired or were defeated in primaries, leading to a relatively quiet general election.[5] About 88 percent of all incumbents were reelected, clearly lower than the

---

[2]Paul R. Abramson, John H. Aldrich, and David W. Rohde, *Change and Continuity in the 1992 Elections* (Washington, DC: Congressional Quarterly Inc., 1994). Herbert F. Weisberg and David C. Kimball, "Attitudinal Correlates of the 1992 Presidential Vote: Party Identification and Beyond," in Herbert F. Weisberg, ed., *Democracy's Feast: Elections in America* (Chatham, NJ: Chatham House, 1995): 72–111.
[3]David Magleby and Kelly Patterson, "The Polls—Poll Trends: Congressional Reform," *Public Opinion Quarterly* 58: 1994: 419–427.
[4]Compare Magleby and Patterson, p. 423, with Kelly Patterson and David Magleby, "Public Support for Congress," *Public Opinion Quarterly* 56(1992): 549.
[5]Gary Jacobson and Michael Dimock, "Checking Out: The Effects of Bank Overdrafts on the 1992 House Elections," *American Journal of Political Science* 38(1994): 601–624.

1980s' average of 95 percent, but a figure not suggestive of any wholesale rejection of Washington.[6] Republicans had put much effort into the redistricting process after the 1990 census and hoped to make significant gains, but in the end they gained only ten seats.

The Senate results were even more disappointing for the Republicans. Twenty of the thirty-five contested seats were held by Democrats. Given that Senate elections in this era are highly competitive and that incumbency counts for less in the Senate than in the House, on statistical grounds alone the Republicans expected to make gains.[7] But when all the votes were counted, the Republicans only broke even, leaving them on the short side of a 57–43 division.

In summary, in 1992 the voting decisions made by millions of Americans brought back unified government, a significant change from the recent past. But a look at the voting decisions that accomplished that result does not reveal major shifts in the way Americans were making their choices. Counting Perot voters, a record 36 percent of those voting split their tickets between the parties' candidates for the presidency and the House. Not counting Perot voters, 22 percent of those voting split their tickets, a figure just three points below the 1972–1988 average.[8]

The 1992 Elections in the States

Arguably, then, if one looked only at the national returns, indications that the era of divided government had ended in 1992 were weak and unclear. In contrast, the picture presented by election returns in the American states was crystal clear: there, the era of divided government continued uninterrupted. The 1990 elections had left only twenty-one states under unified party control; the 1992

[6]Norman Ornstein, Thomas Mann and Michael Malbin, *Vital Statistics on Congress, 1993–94* (Washington, DC: Congressional Quarterly Inc., 1994): Table 2–7.

[7]If every race were a toss-up, then the Republicans would have expected to win 17–18 of the 35 seats. Incumbency would have dampened such expectations somewhat, but the situation still looked highly promising for the Republicans. On statewide competitiveness see Alan Abramowitz and Jeffrey Segal, *Senate Elections* (Ann Arbor, MI: University of Michigan Press, 1995): chapter 8.

[8]These figures are calculated from the 1992 American National Election Study.

elections left twenty states in that condition. The proportion of unified Democratic states barely changed in 1992, and the Republicans continued their abysmal showing of the 1980s by capturing full control in only three states (Arizona, New Hampshire, Utah). They added New Jersey in 1993. These summary figures, moreover, hide what might well be considered a further increase in divided control in the states, for a more detailed examination of patterns of divided control indicates that party control of state legislatures underwent an interesting decline in 1992 (Table 9-1).

The big story of state elections was the upsurge in split legislatures.[9] In discussing Figure 3-5 in Chapter 3, I noted that split legislatures generally numbered 12–18 percent of the total—about eight, give or take a couple. The 1992 elections raised that number to 35 percent of the total—seventeen—far and away the high point of the post-World War II period and perhaps the highest proportion of split legislatures in American history. Moreover, although I remarked (p. 35, note 12) that there was no trend in this indicator, with the addition of the striking 1992 figure there is a clear suggestion of a jump to a new, higher level of split legislatures beginning in 1984, when the number rose to twelve. It has not fallen below that level since. Given that the Supreme Court's one-person one-vote decisions impose strict population equality in constructing both Senate and House districts, the increase in split legislatures since the mid-1980s suggests an increased rate of ticket-splitting in state legislative elections. I am not aware of any research that addresses this question, but it is one that bears investigation.

The split in state legislative control came at the expense of Democratic control (Table 9-2). Before the elections, the Democrats controlled both chambers in 28 states, and the Republicans, both chambers in only 6 states. After the elections, Democrats controlled both chambers in 24 states, while the Republicans controlled both in 8 states. This modest gain in Republican legislative strength in 1992 is noteworthy given that their presidential candidate was going

---

[9]Karl Kurtz of the National Conference on State Legislatures called this to my attention before I had done my own tabulations. Personal communication, March 18, 1993.

Table 9-1   Patterns of Party Control in the States: 1992–1994

Governor	Legislature	1992	1994
Democrat	Democrat	16	8
Republican	Republican	4	15
Democrat	Republican	4	4
Republican	Democrat	7	10
Democrat	Split	8	6
Republican	Split	8	5
Independent	Split	1	1
Independent	Democrat	1	–

Source: Emily Van Dunk and Thomas M. Holbrook, "The 1994 State Legislative Elections." *Extension of Remarks, APSA Legislative Studies Section Newsletter* 18(1994): 8–11.

down to defeat. Whether it foreshadowed in any way their major legislative victories in 1994 is impossible to say, but the development probably deserved more attention than it received.

Table 9-2   Partisan Control of State Legislatures: 1990–1994

	1990	1992	1994
Democratic Chambers	69	64	47
Republican Chambers	25	31	49
Democratic Legislatures	28	24	18
Republican Legislatures	6	8	19

Source: 1990 and 1992 calculated from *Book of the States.* 1994 from Karl Kurtz, "The Tide's In for Southern Republicans." *APSA Legislative Studies Section Newsletter* 18(1994): 9–11.

The 1994 National Elections

Political conditions changed as much between 1992 and 1994 as they had between 1990 and 1992. According to the polls, the electorate that had wavered in its preference for divided over unified national government in the fall of 1992 decided after two years of experience with unified government that divided government was clearly preferable after all (Table 9-3). The relationship between such sentiments and the mid-term congressional voting has not been examined to my knowledge, but, whether out of a preference for divided government or for a host of other reasons, the electorate restored divided national government with the only means at its disposal—electing Republican majorities to Congress.

If the main story of 1992—electoral change—was something of an exaggeration, few will make a similar claim about the main story of 1994—electoral change in the form of the Republican capture of the House of Representatives. Not since 1952 had the Republicans won a majority of House seats, the longest period of one-party control in American history. And not since 1946 had the Republicans received a majority of the nationwide popular vote cast for House candidates. The gain in the party's national popular vote between 1992 and 1994 was 7 percent, not large in absolute terms, but relatively speaking, quite large—tied with 1972–74 as the largest two-year shift in either party's House vote since 1948.[10] With a loss of 53 House seats and eight Senate seats, the "earthquake," "tsunami," and other geological and meteorological metaphors that filled the media were understandable. The House figure in particular was a throwback to the first half of the twentieth century: not since 1948 has a party lost so many seats in one election. Some observers of contemporary House elections never expected to see such a swing in their lifetimes.

Despite the common tendency to paint the Republican victory as a tsunami that washed away all the Democrats in its path, in real-

[10]Everett Carll Ladd, ed., *America at the Polls: 1994* (Storrs, CT: The Roper Institute, 1995): 2. The gain in the Republican aggregate vote between 1990 and 1994 was almost 9 million—the largest midterm-midterm vote gain in American history. See Rhodes Cook, "Rare Combination of Forces May Make History of '94," *Congressional Quarterly Weekly Report* (April 15, 1995): 1077.

Table 9-3 Popular Support for Divided Control

"In general, do you think it is better for the same political party to control both the Congress and the presidency, so they can work together more closely, or do you think it is better to have different political parties controlling the Congress and the presidency, to prevent either one from going too far?"

	Unified	Divided
November 1984	34%	54%
November 1988	32	54
October 1990	23	67
October 1992	39	47
October 1994	36	54

Source: *NBC News/Wall Street Journal* surveys of likely or registered voters. *The Public Perspective*, January/February 1991: 86. *The Public Perspective*, January/February 1993: 108. The Roper Center for Public Opinion Research, University of Connecticut, Storrs, CT

ity, the voting patterns were more complex and their causes more differentiated than such metaphors suggest. The House results had a number of significant components, although as yet there is little research on how important they were and how they interacted with one another:

1. The normal mid-term loss. In every mid-term election since the Civil War except one (1934), the party of the president has lost seats. Given the state of the economy in 1992 (according to the traditional indicators it was pretty good) most statistical forecasting models predicted these "normal" losses to be relatively small. But given Clinton's low approval ratings and the fiasco in Congress created by his health care plan, most analysts expected larger losses.[11]

---

[11]At a panel held during the 1991 American Political Science Association Meetings in Washington, DC, Gary Jacobson, a leading expert on House elections predicted a 20–25 seat loss. This was well before Congress took up health care, and a year before Clinton's approval ratings hit bottom.

2. The secular realignment in the South. The Republicans made their first break-throughs in the South in the 1960s. During the intervening thirty years many southern states had become downright Republican at the presidential level and at least competitive statewide, but the Democrats had been hanging on at the congressional level and holding firm at the state legislative level. The 1994 elections showed significant breakthroughs at these levels.

3. Reapportionment and redistricting. Two distinct factors are at work here. First, following the past two decennial censuses, there has been a reallocation of congressional districts from the frostbelt to the sunbelt—from areas more heavily Democratic to areas relatively less so. In the 1990 reapportionment, sunbelt states gained 18 seats. The second factor is majority-minority redistricting. In recent years Republicans have joined civil rights groups to press for redistricting plans that create the maximum number of seats with African-American and Hispanic majorities. This practice increases the likelihood of electing minority members to Congress but marginally weakens adjacent Democratic seats that lose minority voters. David Lublin estimates that majority-minority redistricting cost the Democrats 13 seats in 1994 (as well as 9 in 1992), an estimate he calls "conservative."[12]

The important point to notice is that losses from these two distinct sources probably should have accrued in 1992, the first election after the census, but the poor showing of George Bush may have enabled some Democrats to hang on in some weakened districts and win in others where they were not expected to. When such districts belatedly fell to the Republicans in 1994, they added to the impression of a national Republican tide.

4. Unpopular issue stands. National Democrats continue to get burned by a variety of symbolic issues on which they are at odds with constituencies who have traditionally supported

---

[12]David Lublin, "Costs of Gerrymandering," letter to the editor, *New York Times*, December, 1994. For elaboration, see Lublin, "Racial Redistricting and the New Republican Majority," unpublished manuscript, 1995.

the Democrats on economic grounds.[13] Such issues contribute to a popular impression that the Democrats are out of step with the values and aspirations of ordinary middle-Americans, an impression the Republicans have been happily exploiting for nearly a generation.

A close look at the congressional voting reveals some important elements of continuity as well as the major instances of change that we have noted. In particular, 90 percent of all running House incumbents were reelected, a slight increase over 1992, although 5 percent below the average of the previous decade. The incumbent reelection rate in 1994 was higher than the *average* for the elections between 1946 and 1966, suggesting that, even in 1994, incumbency is of a different order of importance than it was a generation ago. To be sure, with the electoral tide running in the Republican direction not a single Republican incumbent lost, while 33 Democratic incumbents did. The latter is an unusually large number but one that still left the Democrats with an 85 percent success rate. Using one widely accepted method of calculation, the incumbency advantage in 1994 was about 12 percent for Republicans, about 8 percent for Democrats; the advantage of incumbency certainly did not disappear in 1994.[14]

In the Senate, the Republicans also enjoyed great success, although their takeover there was much less of a surprise. For the second election in a row, the Democrats were heavily exposed in Senate races: 22 of the 35 seats up for election in 1994 were held by Democrats. Given that Senate races have become highly competitive

[13]For example, gun control is an issue that is poison in southern and western states and even in states like Pennsylvania where the NRA has 200,000 members. While I have no systematic evidence on this point, my reading of campaign reports and conversations with various local observers suggest that gun control may have been the difference in at least a half dozen seats in 1994, including the defeats of long-time incumbents like Jack Brooks (TX), and Dan Glickman (KS). For a comprehensive treatment of the gun control issue see Robert Spitzer, *The Politics of Gun Control* (Chatham, NJ: Chatham House, 1995).

[14]The method is set forth in Andrew Gelman and Gary King, "Estimating the Incumbency Advantage Without Bias," *American Journal of Political Science* 34(1142–64). Thanks to Gary King for the 1994 figures.

in recent years, many observers thought it possible that the Republicans would gain enough seats to win control, despite their failure to do so when the Democrats were similarly exposed in 1992. The Republicans needed a net gain of seven seats but got eight (plus Richard Shelby of Alabama who defected from the Democrats shortly after the election). Only two Democratic incumbents lost, but every single open seat was captured by the Republicans.

Whatever the policy consequences of the Republican victories (and at the time of this writing it is too early to tell what they will be), the 1994 election results make it clear that the Democratic lock on the House of Representatives has been broken. Taken in combination with the 1992 results in which the Democrats at least picked the Republican lock on the presidency, these two most recent elections indicate that either party can capture any one of the three branches of the national government given circumstances that we have seen transpire in a three or four year span of time. This suggests that divided government at the national level will be common in years to come, although it may take patterns different from the Republican president/Democratic Congress that became the norm between 1968 and 1992. In particular, the present division of Democratic president/Republican Congress is the first instance of such a pattern since 1946.

The 1994 Elections in the States

And what of the states in 1994? There, too, the Republicans made great gains. About three-quarters of the states elect their governors in the mid-term elections, so this office was highly exposed to the Republican tide. The Republicans did very well, winning 24 of 36 races, giving them control of a majority of the governorships for the first time since the halcyon days of 1966–68, although there had been other, more recent elections (1980 and 1986) in which they had also done relatively well (Figure 3-4).

However one characterizes the Republican gubernatorial gains, their gains at the state legislative level were striking (Table 9-2). They gained a total of 18 chambers, taking full control of 19 legislatures to the Democrats' 18. This is the largest number of legislatures the

Republicans have controlled since 1968, and the first time since 1954 that they have controlled more legislatures than the Democrats have.

Despite the great Republican gains, however, there was little or no increase in unified control in the states (Table 9-1). From 20 states before the elections, the number of unified states rose to only 23 after the 1994 elections. The parties flopped positions, of course; the Republicans controlled only 4 states before the election and 15 after, whereas the Democrats dropped from 16 to 8, so the changes largely offset each other. The level of divided government in the states today is basically unchanged from the historical low point reached in the late 1980s (compare Figure 3-1 with Table 9-1). Republican governor/Democratic legislature continues to be the single most common divided pattern, but it has declined in frequency in recent years as the number of split legislatures has increased. In 1994 the number of split legislatures dropped back from its record 1992 level to 12, a figure still on the high side of the historical norm.

The other noteworthy development in 1994 was the Republican state legislative breakthrough in the South. In Chapter 3, I observed that between 1946 and 1990 the Republicans had never won control of either chamber of a state legislature in any southern or border state. In 1994, they broke through with majorities in the Florida Senate and North Carolina and South Carolina Houses. Few observers are betting that this is a fluke; more likely it is only the opening wedge for further Republican gains.

In summary, a Republican tide clearly rolled across the states in 1994. That tide produced major changes in party control of governorships and state legislative chambers. Somewhat surprisingly, however, the Republican surge did little to alter the overall distribution of party control in the states. Many unified Democratic states were pushed into the various divided categories, and many divided states were pushed into the unified Republican category (Figure 9-1), but on net the divided category stayed about the same size. Thus, in the states, the era of divided government continues uninterrupted.

Conclusion

Indisputably, 1992 and 1994 were interesting elections. Change in control of the presidency for the first time in twelve years is news;

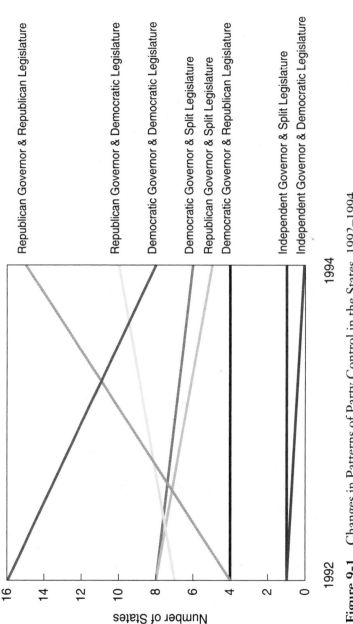

Figure 9-1   Changes in Patterns of Party Control in the States, 1992–1994

change in control of the House of Representatives for the first time in forty years is big news. But I would argue that the major lesson of these elections is that the era of divided government continues. At the national level, a quasi-stable pattern of Republican presidents/Democratic Congresses may have broken down, but it is now clear that 1992 did not herald a return to an era of unified Democratic government, and it is far too early to tell whether 1994 foreshadows a new era of unified Republican government. My suspicion is that recent national developments indicate that we have now entered a period in which divided government will continue to be frequent, but it will occur in a richer variety of patterns of control than the Republican President/Democratic Congress pattern of the past generation.

As for the states, nothing has changed. A look at patterns of control in these 50 separate political systems reveals no indication that the 1992 and 1994 elections broke the tendency toward divided control that had become apparent during the past generation. The Republicans certainly are stronger now than at any time since 1968, and the decline of Republican fortunes in state legislative elections has, at the least, been arrested. But Republican gains have not been matched by increases in unified control given that such gains have been offset by declines in unified Democratic control.

Indeed, in the states, too, we are seeing not only as much divided control as in recent years, but a richer variety of patterns as well. In particular, the increase in split state legislatures indicates that the common divided pattern of Republican governor/Democratic legislature has given way to more complicated patterns in which the legislature, too, is split. Interestingly, recent work by Alt and Lowrey finds that divided control of state government that involves a split between the executive and legislative branches has less of an effect on a state's capacity to deal with fiscal difficulties than divided control that involves a split legislature.[15] Hence, at least in the fiscal realm, the recent rise in split legislative control may be a negative development in that states whose legislatures are in opposite party hands will have greater difficulty in handling fiscal pressures that are currently quite widespread.

[15]James Alt and Robert Lowrey, "Divided Government, Fiscal Institutions, and Budget Deficits: Evidence from the States," *American Political Science Reveiw* 88(1994): 811–828.

RECENT RESEARCH ON THE CAUSES
OF DIVIDED GOVERNMENT

Chapters 4 and 5 discussed a number of factors that might have contributed to the increase in divided government during the past generation. I divided these possible contributing factors into two kinds:

accidental, wherein some development in the political system might have contributed to divided control in an indirect and unforeseen way, and

intentional, wherein voters might be acting with some degree of purpose to bring about divided control.

Both kinds of explanations have been the subject of recent research. As is commonly the case in the early stages of a research program, disagreements abound. But while definitive explanations of divided government are still some time in the future, it is fair to say that we know a bit more now than we did several years ago.

Research on Accidental Explanations

As noted in Chapter 3, the sources of the decline in unified state government can be located more precisely in two senses. First, in a partisan sense, the decline was one in unified *Republican* state government—although unified Democratic control fluctuated considerably, there was no trend across the period (Figure 3-3). In contrast, several times in the early post-war period, the Republicans were able to capture a majority of the non-southern states, but by the 1990s their strongholds could be measured in the low single digits—only three states in 1990 and 1992.

The sources of the decline in unified state government also could be located more precisely in a second, institutional, sense. There was no apparent erosion in the Republican capacity to contest gubernatorial elections (Figure 3-4). In fact, given aggregate party identification estimates for the states, Republican gubernatorial candidates appeared to enjoy success disproportionate to the percentage of Republican identifiers in their state electorates. It was in the *legislatures* that Republican fortunes eroded (Figure 3-5). From control in a majority of states in the early post-war period, Republican control collapsed to single digit levels by the 1990s—five state legislatures in 1990, eight in 1992. Interestingly, adjusting for the series of Democratic landslides (1958, 1964, 1974) that are reflections of national conditions, most of the deterioration in Republican legislative fortunes seemed to have occurred in the 1960s, give or take a few years in either direction. By the mid-1970s, Democratic legislative fortunes had reached a plateau. This temporal pattern is evident in both the graph of legislative control (Figure 3-5) and in a graph of the number of Democratic state legislators (Figure 10-1).

In Chapter 4, I suggested that the preceding changes in state legislative elections might be related to the advent of legislative professionalism. In the early post-war period most state legislatures were what legislative scholars call *amateur* legislatures—part-time, minimally staffed, and minimally compensated. State constitutions often limited legislatures to meeting biennially rather than annually, and also severely constrained the term during which they might sit. A forty- to sixty-day session limit was common, and even a legislature permitted to meet annually might be constrained to a short (e.g., twenty day) session every second year. Legislative compensation was commensurate with these modest responsibilities. Not surprisingly, under such conditions turnover was often as high as 50 percent per election and was more the product of voluntary retirement than of electoral competition.

During the past forty years, many state legislatures moved away from such an amateur concept toward the *professional* model represented by Congress—full-time, heavily staffed, and respectably com-

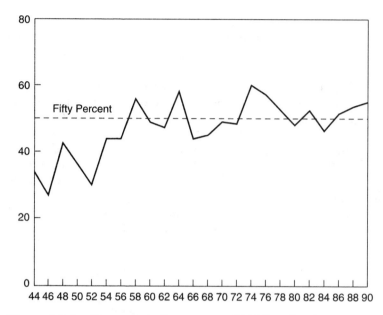

Figure 10-1   Democratic Percentage of 31 Non-Southern
Legislatures

pensated.[1] Few state legislatures can match the standard offered by
Congress, of course, but legislatures in a number of our larger states
are clearly professional bodies, and in many states there are far more
professional legislators than before.[2] Over three-quarters of the state
legislatures now meet annually, session lengths have increased
steadily, compensation has risen dramatically, and member turnover
has declined. Importantly, the movement toward legislative professionalism was a northern phenomenon, as was the decline in Republican legislative control. All of the Republican legislative decline
came in the non-south: until 1994, the Republicans never had a

[1]Karl Kurtz, *Understanding the Diversity of State Legislatures: The Red, White, and Blue
Legislatures.* (Denver, CO: National Conference of State Legislatures, 1991).
[2]For example, Bazar notes that in the Middle Atlantic States more than half the
legislators were self-designated full-timers by the mid-1980s. See Beth Bazar, *State
Legislators' Occupations: A Decade of Change.* (Denver, CO: National Conference of
State Legislatures, 1987).

southern or border legislature (or even one chamber of a legislature) to lose. Similarly, most of the gain in professionalism came in the non-south. Today none of the southern and border states are considered to be professionalized.[3]

When one examines common indicators of legislative professionalism, the temporal coincidence between growth in professionalism and deterioration in Republican legislative control is highly suggestive. The number of states with annual sessions doubled in the 1950s and doubled again in the 1960s with an especially sharp rise between 1968 and 1972 (Figure 10-2). By the mid-1970s, more than 80 percent of the non-southern states had annual sessions, with little change thereafter.

The picture is somewhat different for the number of days per session during which a legislature sits (Figure 10-3). Here there is a

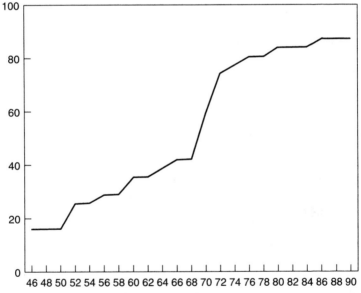

Figure 10-2   Percentage of 31 Non-Southern States with Annual Sessions

[3]None of them fall into the "red" category in the classification offered by Kurtz.

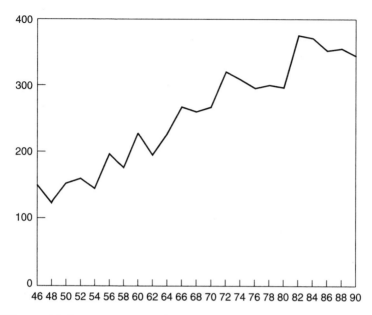

Figure 10-3   Average Number of Days in Session in 31 Non-
Southern Legislatures

more nearly linear increase. In the late 1950s, the average non-
southern state legislature sat for a little under 200 days every two
years. By the early 1970s, the average had increased to over 300.
Some legislatures are much like Congress—virtually always in session. In Massachusetts, for example, the legislature has sat for at
least 700 days in every two-year period since 1982.

As legislative service became more time intensive, compensation
naturally increased accordingly. With the legislature in session for
200–300 days every year, few legislators could engage in outside
occupations; increasingly, they looked to legislative service as their
principal source of income. In the early post-war period when the
amateur concept dominated, average legislative compensation was
less than real per capita disposable income, but compensation
increased dramatically throughout the 1960s, finally halting as stagflation gripped the country in the mid-1970s (Figure 10-4).

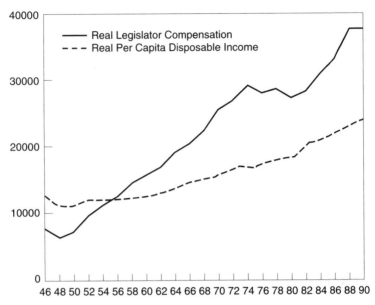

Figure 10-4   Average Biennial Compensation *versus* per Capita
Disposable Income in 31 Non-Southern States (1980
Dollars)

Ironically, the professionalization movement in some ways is the
reverse of the current terms limitation movement. A generation ago,
reformers believed that turnover in state legislatures was too high, not
too low. Many thought that the demands of the modern age necessi-
tated more capable legislators who would serve long enough to accrue
knowledge and experience that would be conducive to effective lawmaking. Hence, legislatures should be made into full-time bodies with
compensation sufficient to attract "professional" legislators. Appropriate reforms were proposed by good government groups such as the
National Municipal League, League of Women Voters, and the Citizens Conference on State Legislatures, and the professional expertise
of political scientists contributed to the reform effort.[4]

[4]Alexander Heard, *State Legislatures in American Politics* (Englewood Cliffs: Prentice-
Hall, 1966).

My own research since the first edition suggests that the development of legislative professionalism indeed contributed significantly to the drop in Republican control of state legislatures.[5] Specifically, controlling statistically for state electoral histories, temporal trends, national economic conditions, presidential and gubernatorial coattails, and obvious socio-demographic variables (state population, income, and expenditures), each $10,000 increase in real biennial legislator compensation is associated with about a 1 percent increase in Democratic representatives in the non-southern states.[6] That is the *direct* contribution; there is an additional indirect contribution through the increase over time in the size of the Democratic base. To mention a specific example, real legislator compensation in California has increased ninefold in the post-war period, an increase that translated directly into a jump of 9 percent in the size of the Democratic House contingent.

Why should legislative professionalism advantage Democrats relative to Republicans? As discussed in Chapter 4, the logic is not partisan, or even political, in a broader sense. Rather, the answer may be simply that different kinds of candidates self-select into amateur and professional legislatures.

Service in an amateur legislature presumes another, primary, source of income. Moreover, that livelihood must not be jeopardized by serving one to three months a year in government. Thus, professionals and proprietors with flexible schedules, farmers and ranchers with little to do in the winter, and spouses of the same are well situated to serve in amateur legislatures. In contrast, those whose livelihoods consist of wages and salaries for fixed hours worked are effectively precluded from service. Amateur legislatures advantage those whose occupations allow them the flexibility to combine public service and private careers—people in Republican-leaning occupational categories.

---

[5]This research is described in detail in "Divided Government in the American States: A Byproduct of Legislative Professionalism?" *American Political Science Review* 88(1994): 304–316.

[6]Legislator compensation includes salaries, *per diems* and other allowances—anything that could be reliably calculated. Session lengths also were included in the statistical analysis but real compensation proved to be much the stronger indicator. Of course, session lengths are related to compensation. See *ibid.*, for details.

In professional legislatures, a reverse logic operates. Professional legislatures require an individual to give up outside occupations, become full-time legislators, and live on the associated compensation. For many Republicans, the "opportunity costs" of abandoning lucrative outside careers are higher than the benefits of legislative service. In contrast, a professional legislature may be an attractive alternative for individuals employed in the lower-salaried public and non-profit sectors—people in Democratic-leaning occupational groups.

Thus, as legislative session lengths rise, potential Republican candidates find the prospect of service less attractive. Although compensation is rising simultaneously, it is not sufficient to replace income from their outside occupations. Conversely, as compensation rises, prospective Democratic candidates regard legislative service as an increasingly attractive prospect; on average the returns from their outside occupations are not as generous as those enjoyed by Republicans. I emphasize that there is no need to argue that public service is simply a matter of wages and hours, only to point out that, at the margins, wages and hours do affect the political calculations of prospective candidates. The most public-spirited Democrat may be financially unable to survive on the compensation provided by an amateur legislature, just as the most public-spirited Republican may be unwilling to make the sacrifice required by a professional legislature.

Although there is no direct evidence as yet that such personal career calculations are indeed what drove the decline in Republican fortunes, the statistical evidence for the association of the two trends is quite solid. An alternative, more ideological, hypothesis is that Democrats like government and so are willing to serve full time, whereas Republicans dislike government and will not serve full time. This hypothesis is not incompatible with the opportunity cost hypothesis I have offered, but, in the statistical analysis, "days in session" was much less strongly related to declining Republican fortunes than was compensation, although the two variables of course are related.

What of the 1994 results discussed in the preceding chapter? Do they indicate that some new dynamic is now at work, a dynamic that will erode the favorable Democratic legislative equilibrium established in the 1970s? It is far too early to tell, but I am somewhat

doubtful. The statistical analysis of the effects of legislative professionalism also found strong effects for presidential and gubernatorial
coattails, and a striking mid-term reaction against the party of the
incumbent president. Specifically, a party's percentage of lower-
house state legislators was predicted to rise by about .4 percent for
every percent of the vote over 50 percent that its gubernatorial candidate draws. Furthermore, a party is predicted to gain about 10 percent of the state legislative seats in the mid-term elections when the
presidency is held by the other party. Thus, the Democratic presidency and the strong showing of Republican gubernatorial candidates were predicted to make 1994 a banner year for Republicans in
state legislative races. All their political stars were in proper align-
ment.

Research on Purposive Explanations

Chapter 5 discussed a number of purposive explanations for the
split-ticket voting that underlies contemporary patterns of divided
control. These have in common the idea that some voters, perhaps
unconsciously, are engaging in some kind of balancing act when they
vote, leaning toward one party when voting for the executive but
countering that vote with a different one when voting for legislators.
Voters could be balancing off Democratic competence in domestic
policy against Republican competence in foreign and macroeco-
nomic policy as suggested by Gary Jacobson, or balancing off conservative Republicans with liberal Democrats as I had suggested
earlier, or even voting for gridlock when both parties seemed corrupt and untrustworthy. The policy or ideological balancing model,
in particular, has stimulated a lively controversy.

Policy Balancing

In Chapter 5 (p. 76) I observed that *ceteris paribus* balancing models
predict that ticket-splitting would be most common among people
between the two parties—moderates, relatively speaking, and noted
that the evidence was consistent with that prediction (note 22). I did
not make much of the finding since it seemed so obvious. Moreover,

other logics would also suggest that people between the parties are more likely to split. For example, people between the parties might view them as equally good or bad and consequently would be indifferent between them. It would not be surprising if such "indifferents" scattered their votes among candidates of both parties.

Somewhat surprisingly, Alvarez and Schousen (1993) find that this prediction is not upheld when looking at voter and candidate placements in the 1972–1988 American National Election Studies.[7] Born, who is otherwise critical of balancing models, reports more positive findings, although they are not statistically significant.[8] Garand and Lichtl report stronger positive findings for the 1992 national elections.[9] They also find that people who express an abstract preference for divided over unified government are more likely to split their ticket, although this effect is contingent on voters' having a certain level of political knowledge.

Only Born has attempted to assess the other predictions generated by the policy balancing model. He finds that the "pattern prediction" (pp. 78–79) that specifies *how* the voter will split her vote between president and House is clearly supported by the data both at the individual and aggregate levels.[10] He also attempts to test the dynamic predictions of the model—for example, that increasing polarization will lead to increasing ticket-splitting, *ceteris paribus* (pp. 77–78). He views the results as generally negative, while I view them as generally positive, but, since the tests are based on variation across only five election studies (1972–1988) all of which come *after* the sharp rise in national ticket-splitting, the findings are inconclusive.[11]

Along somewhat different lines, Borelli reports mixed results for ideological balancing models in explaining state divided govern-

[7]Michael Alvarez and Matthew Schousen, "Policy Moderation or Conflicting Expectations. Testing the Intentional Models of Split Ticket Voting," *American Politics Quarterly* 21(1993): 410–438.

[8]Richard Born, "Split Ticket Voters, Divided Government, and Fiorina's Policy-Balancing Model," *Legislative Studies Quarterly* 19(1994): 95–115.

[9]James Garand and Marci Glascock Lichtl, "Explaining Divided Government: Testing an Intentional Model of Split-Ticket Voting," forthcoming.

[10]Born, pp. 107–08.

[11]Morris Fiorina, "Response to Born," *Legislative Studies Quarterly* 19(1994): 117–125.

ment.[12] Alesina and Rosenthal find temporal balancing models (on-year to off-term) useful in explaining the results of mid-term national elections.[13] Finally, Schmidt, Kenny and Morton report clear support for balancing in Senate elections, as sketched on pp. 81–84.[14] Other things being equal, Senators running for reelection between 1962 and 1990 did from 5–17 percent better when the sitting Senator not up for reelection was a member of the other party.

All in all, the empirical support for the kind of policy balancing model sketched in Chapter 5 is mixed. I would agree with Borelli's assessment that such models remain "in the ring."[15] Many colleagues believe that such models make too severe informational demands on the voter. But I never advanced such a model as an explanation of *all* ticket-splitting. About 25 percent of the voters split their tickets between presidential and House decisions. About one-third of them fall into the high information category where Garand and Lichtl find evidence for purposive ticket-splitting. That means about 8 percent of the voters could be engaging in intentional behavior. A net shift of about that size turned American politics on its head in 1994.

Policy Consistency

Paul Frymer has advanced an interesting alternative to a policy-balancing model.[16] He argues that much presidential-House ticket-splitting reflects consistent policy or ideological voting rather than

[12]Stephen Borrelli, "Party Polarization, Ideological Balancing, and Divided Government in the American States," forthcoming.

[13]Alberto Alesina and Howard Rosenthal, "Partisan Cycles in Congressional Elections and the Macroeconomy," *American Political Science Review* 83(1989): 373–398.

[14]Amy Schmidt, Lawrence Kenny and Rebecca Morton, "Evidence on Electoral Accountability in the U.S. Senate: Are Unfaithful Agents Really Punished?" *Economic Inquiry*, forthcoming.

[15]Borelli, p. 13.

[16]Paul Frymer, "Ideological Consensus within Divided Party Government," *Political Science Quarterly* 109(1994): 287–311. Deborah Jordan Brooks independently formulated a similar model. See her "Toward an Ideological Model of the Split-Ticket Voter," excerpt from senior honors thesis, UC Santa Cruz, 1993).

balancing. Specifically, in districts that cast majorities for Reagan or Bush and Democratic House incumbents, the incumbent representatives tend to come from the conservative wing of the Democratic Party, and the bigger the majority for the Republican president, the more conservative the Democratic incumbent. Thus, voters splitting their ticket might be voting consistently for a conservative president-House pair. This argument certainly deserves consideration, but there is a critical ambiguity in the empirical relationship that Frymer uses to support it.

Implicitly, Frymer assumes a situation that resembles the top panel in Figure 10-5. In this situation a vote for Reagan and a vote for the Democratic member of Congress are both votes for the identical conservative position. This is clearly ideologically consistent ticket-splitting. Note however, that to measure a member's ideology by ADA (Americans for Democratic Action) or *National Journal* scores is to measure her position relative to her fellow members of Congress. That position tells us nothing about where she fits on the ideological spectrum in her district.[17] Thus, the situation could just as easily resemble the middle panel of Figure 10-5. Here, although the Democratic incumbent is still conservative relative to the national Democrats (represented by Mondale), she is more liberal than the Republican candidate in her district, who takes the same position as Reagan. Here, Reagan/Democratic ticket-splitting would not be ideologically consistent. And, of course, we can have other situations that are combinations of these two, where we can not determine whether ticket-splitting is ideologically consistent. In the bottom panel of Figure 10-5, a straight Republican vote would involve supporting a Republican House candidate exactly as far from the president as the Democratic House candidate, but in the opposite direction. If the voter's own position lies to the right of Reagan, a straight Republican vote is ideologically consistent; if the voter's own position lies to the left of Reagan, but to the right of the Democratic House candidate, a Republican president/Democratic House split is ideologically consistent. Without knowing where the voter stands, we can not classify his vote.

---

[17]Morris Fiorina, *Representatives, Roll Calls, and Constituencies* (Lexington, MA: Heath, 1974): 19–23.

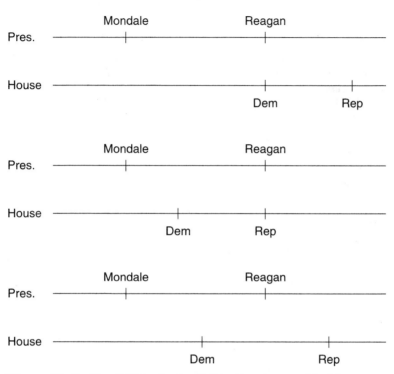

Figure 10-5 Possibilities in the Policy Consistency Model

Thus, unless we have data on both the Democratic incumbent and her Republican challenger, and unless we can put the presidential candidates and the voters on the same scale, we cannot differentiate among such different situations and hence decide whether ticket-splitting is consistent with an ideological consistency or ideological balancing model. The consistency model clearly deserves investigation, but it will be as difficult to put it to a definitive test as to test the balancing model.

A Pox on Both Your Houses? Balancing Undesirables

Chapter 5 also takes note of arguments that ticket-splitting may represent a voter's desire to check one corrupt or otherwise undesirable party with another. Although I have encountered a fair amount of anecdotal evidence consistent with such behavior, my own preliminary research turned up little by way of consistent evidence. The less trusting, more alienated voters were sometimes more likely to split their tickets, sometimes less, sometimes equally so. But in what is clearly the best-controlled empirical study to date, Garand and Lichtl find that low trust was significantly associated with ticket-splitting in 1992.[18] Thus, the bottom line here seems again to be that the hypothesis is "in the ring." We need replications of the Garand-Lichtl study for other election years before we can draw any firm conclusions.

An Observation about 1996

If balancing models have any empirical footing, the Republican victories in the 1994 Congressional elections have raised the probability that President Clinton will be reelected in 1996.

Conclusion

Research on the causes of divided government has only begun, but it has already produced some interesting findings and stimulated several lively controversies. In part, divided control may result from structural or otherwise nonpolitical features of political processes and/or institutions that advantage one party relative to the other. An example appears to be the 1960s-1970s professionalization of state legislatures that lessened their attractiveness to Republicans and increased their attractiveness to Democrats, thus presenting the northern electorate with fewer and/or less-attractive Republican candidates today than a generation ago. If the governorship did not change in its relative attractiveness to candidates of the two parties, the expected result would be a decline in Republican legislative fortunes unaccompanied by any corresponding decline in gubernatorial fortunes.

[18]Garand and Lichtl, Tables 4–7.

But divided control also may have more directly political causes. A second line of inquiry has investigated the causes of split-ticket voting, in particular, whether there exists any indication that ticket-splitters are motivated by some sort of balancing logic that leads them to distribute their votes across the two parties' candidates. It has been difficult to find statistically significant evidence for this popular impression in the most widely available collections of survey data, but some positive evidence has been uncovered, and research continues.

THE CONSEQUENCES OF DIVIDED
GOVERNMENT REVISITED

During the 1992 presidential campaign a new issue came to the fore. It was not a policy issue such as reducing the deficit or "ending welfare as we know it," or admitting homosexuals into the military. Nor was it an issue of personal or institutional performance such as President Bush's handling of the economy or the apparent venality of Congress. The issue was broader than either policy or performance; the issue was *gridlock*. According to many commentators—by no means all of them Democrats—the United States had taken a long look at Sundquist's "new era of coalition government" and, like him, they found it wanting.[1] Years of Republican presidents cohabiting with Democratic Congresses had generated an indictment that charged divided government with "bitter partisanship, poor governmental performance, policy incoherence, nondecisions, showdowns, standoffs, checkmate, stalemate, deadlock, and, in the most recent nomenclature, *gridlock*."[2]

In Chapter 6 I noted that there was little empirical support for the strong claims that have been made about the negative effects of divided control. Whether one looked closely at deficits, at legislative productivity, at inter-branch conflict, at presidents' ability to conduct foreign affairs or staff their administrations, there was little in

---

[1]James Sundquist, "Needed: A Political Theory for the New Era of Coalition Government in the United States," *Political Science Quarterly* 103(1988): 613–35.
[2]This pithy summation of the bill of particulars aimed at divided government is due to Keith Krehbiel, "Institutional and Partisan Sources of Gridlock: A Theory of Divided and Unified Government," *Journal of Theoretical Politics*, forthcoming, 1996.

the empirical record that pointed to significant differences between years of unified government and years of split control. That may have been the case as of 1988 but had the picture changed during the Bush administration? Had the divided-government chickens finally come home to roost? Many Democrats suggested as much, many pundits agreed with them, and even voters became less supportive of divided government than they had been earlier (Table 9-3).

Efficiency and Effectiveness under Unified Government: The Experience of 1993–94

When Bill Clinton was elected, advocates of activist government breathed a sigh of relief. With unified control restored, the country could once again expect innovative programs, decisive government action, and efficient institutional performance. Such expectations were not just the exaggerated expectations of naïve observers. Experienced Congressional leaders convinced President-elect Clinton that he should ignore moderate Republicans and adopt a legislative strategy that relied exclusively on the Democratic majorities in Congress. For his own part, Clinton imprudently announced that he expected his first 100 days to be the most productive period since Franklin Roosevelt.[3]

Things do not seem to have worked out that way. Almost immediately, President Clinton was slapped down by Congress when he expressed his intention to issue an executive order ending discrimination against homosexuals by the military. Not only did his own party not stand behind him, they rallied to a "Don't ask, don't tell" alternative offered by Senator Sam Nunn (D-GA) that fell far short of Clinton's proposal.[4] This was hardly an auspicious beginning. The finale of his first two years was far worse. Health care reform, the planned centerpiece of the Clinton administration, died a long, noisy, and messy death in Congress, some months after the Con-

---

[3]He also observed that Abraham Lincoln and Woodrow Wilson were elected with majorities smaller than his, a somewhat immodest comparison.

[4]Pat Towell, "Campaign Promise, Social Debate Collide on Military Battlefield," *Congressional Quarterly Weekly Report*, January 20, 1993: 226–229.

gressional Democrats rejected the President's plan and attempted to substitute various ones of their own.

In between, there was considerably more of the same. Many of the president's victories recalled the "Perils of Pauline" stories of the silent movie era. His budget passed by a single vote in the House, as conservative Democrats abandoned ship. The president won on NAFTA (North American Free Trade Agreement) only because Republican Speaker-to-Be Newt Gingrich delivered the Republican votes to make up for Democratic defections. Dissident Democrats joined with Republicans to hold up the crime bill, forcing the president to make concessions on spending. A Democratic Senator, Fritz Hollings, held up a vote on GATT (General Agreement on Tariffs and Trade) until after the 1994 elections, at which time President Clinton was forced into embarrassing negotiations with the newly empowered Republican minority. But on these matters Clinton won in the end at least, however difficult and politically damaging the process.

Other policy-making episodes did not have happy endings. The President's economic stimulus package died in the Senate as the strategy of relying exclusively on Democratic votes in Congress encouraged Republicans to adopt a "take no prisoners" approach to the president's program. The campaign finance reform package also died in the Senate, but not before complacent House Democrats had delayed it for a year. The Congress rejected the president's proposal to reform grazing rights in the West, and Superfund died as well. Environmentalists labeled the 103rd Congress a disappointment.[5]

Faced with such developments, the high hopes expressed only two years earlier turned to disappointment. Rank-and-file House Democrats rushed to adjourn, suggesting the desire to get out of Washington before they did any further political damage.[6] Polls found that voters once again overwhelmingly saw the virtues of divided control (Table 9-3). Some in the media could scarcely contain their disgust.

[5]David S. Cloud, "Health Care's Painful Demise Cast Pall on Clinton Agenda," *Congressional Quarterly Weekly Report*, November 5, 1994: 3144.
[6]David S. Cloud, "End of Session Marked by Partisan Stalemate," *Congressional Quarterly Weekly Report*, October 8, 1994: 2849

This will go down in the record books as perhaps the worst Congress—least effective, most destructive, nastiest—in 50 years. The wisdom of the moment is that the dismal record represents a victory for the Republicans...But it's also a myth to claim that they bear the entire responsibility for the failure that has occurred. The Democrats brought a major part of the wreckage on themselves...The only good news as this mud fight finally winds down is that it's hard to imagine much worse.[7]

Things were not as bad as that. The disappointment and disillusion expressed in late 1994 were no more justified than the hope and anticipation expressed in late 1992. Unified government should not have been expected to work miracles, and a fair review of the record suggests that unified control in 1993–94 was by no means the disaster suggested by some.

David Mayhew has updated the research reviewed in Chapter 6 and on that basis judges the 103rd Congress as "relatively productive.... good...respectable.... I think with five years' perspective we'll say this is an average first Congress for a president.... It's like Truman's first Congress, or Carter's first, maybe a little bigger than Kennedy's first."[8] To be sure, Mayhew by no means was retreating from his earlier conclusion that divided government was equally as productive as unified government. He goes on to say that "Once you step back and look, you wonder whether it adds up to more than Bush's first Congress.... I don't think it's in a class with Ronald Reagan's first Congress."[9]

Contrary to much of what has been written and said in the media, most academic observers of Congress judge that the two years of unified government under Clinton were reasonably productive. In addition to deficit reduction, NAFTA, and GATT, one finds (amidst the various defeats and embarrassments) significant policy

---

[7]"Perhaps the Worst Congress," *Washington Post National Weekly Edition,* October 17–23, 1994: 27.

[8]Stephen Gettinger, "View from the Ivory Tower More Rosy than Media's," *Congressional Quarterly Weekly Report,* October 8, 1994: 2850.

[9]Ibid. See also David Mayhew, "The Return to Unified Party Control Under Clinton: How Much of a Difference in Lawmaking?" in Bryan D. Jones, ed., *The New American Politics* (Boulder, CO: Westview Press, 1995): 111–121.

initiatives such as the Family and Medical Leave Act, the National Service Corps, the Brady (handgun control) bill, and the Crime bill, as well as procedural reforms such as "motor voter" registration, Hatch Act revisions, and reform of government procurement. Moreover, scholars such as Charles O. Jones and James Thurber point out "negative" accomplishments such as termination of giant pork barrel projects like the superconducting super collider.[10]

All in all, the lessons to be drawn from the 1993–94 episode of unified national control appear quite consistent with those drawn from previous episodes. There were plenty of instances of gridlock and stalemate but also instances of legislative accomplishment. Despite hyperbolic newspaper editorials and bitter partisan commentary, the experience of the 103rd Congress suggests no need to revise the earlier conclusion of Chapter 6. This episode of unified government seems well within the historical range of what one could expect from either a unified or a divided government. But this is an admittedly impressionistic judgment. What does more recent systematic research indicate?

Divided Government and Legislative Productivity: Recent Research

Mayhew Revisited

Sean Kelley is not as persuaded by Mayhew's study as many other analysts are.[11] Recall that Mayhew identified significant legislation via two "sweeps" of alternative sources. Sweep 1 was based on the judgments of contemporary journalists writing the year-end wrap-ups in *The New York Times* and *The Washington Post*. Sweep 2 was based on the retrospective judgments of policy analysts writing about their particular areas of expertise. Any enactment identified in either sweep is part of Mayhew's compilation of significant legislation. Kelley proposes that significant legislation be defined not as the union of both sweeps but rather as their intersection. If a pro-

[10]Ibid.
[11]"Divided We Govern: A Reassessment," *Polity* 25(1993): 475–484.

posal were not considered important at the time, what does it matter if it becomes significant later as a result of changing conditions or unforeseen consequences? Conversely, if a proposal proves to be an ineffective or inappropriate remedy, what does it matter if journalists thought it important at the time? Promise and performance are each necessary conditions for legislation to be judged significant, and they should be weighted equally.[12] Kelley shows that, using this more stringent definition of significant legislation, periods of divided control indeed produce fewer significant pieces of legislation than periods of unified control, about six enactments per Congress in the former condition as compared with about nine in the latter—not the difference between paralysis and paradise to be sure, but a difference that is statistically significant at conventional levels. Mayhew remains unconvinced, feeling that his either-or procedure takes better account of biases in the way political journalists view legislative output.[13]

Adler and Cameron go in the opposite direction from Kelley, expanding the notion of important legislation rather than contracting it.[14] Pointing out that the "historic milestones" in the year-end newspaper wrap-ups constitute only 1.3 percent of all the bills passed by Congress between 1947 and 1992, Adler and Cameron loosen the definition of important legislation to include any bill mentioned in the year-end wrap-ups. This lowering of standards of importance still results in less than 5 percent of Congressional enactments being classified as "major."[15]

Adler and Cameron subject this expanded set of enactments to an impressive empirical analysis that includes both demand-side (public opinion, socio-economic conditions) and supply-side (political and institutional) variables. Their conclusions are rich and not easy to summarize, but for present purposes the most important one

[12]Ibid., 478.

[13]"Response: Let's Stick with the Longer List," *Polity* 25(1993): 489–490.

[14]E. Scott Adler and Charles M. Cameron, "The Macro-Politics of Congress: The Enactment of Significant Legislation 1947–1992, forthcoming,

[15]It is rather interesting to learn that 18 percent of Congressional enactments are too minor to receive newspaper notice (although they receive mention in the *Congressional Quarterly Almanacs;* that 63 percent of enactments are "non-substantive," (they even escape the notice of *Congressional Quarterly*); and that the remaining 13 percent are "trivial" (mostly commemorative).

is that the "findings strongly confirm Mayhew's conclusion and extend it to a broader class of significant legislation: simple models of divided versus unified party government are poor tools for understanding the enactment of important laws."[16]

General Treatments of Legislative Productivity

Although their approaches and methodologies could not be more different, important recent studies by Charles Jones and Keith Krehbiel reach very similar overall conclusions.[17] Based on an extensive, empirical study of post-World War II presidents, Jones finds that divided government is only one of many factors that determine legislative productivity and other measures of presidential success. Indeed, split-party control may not even be a major factor in many cases. Only when it occurs in combination with other considerations does divided control have the popularly assumed negative effects.

Jones identifies four patterns of presidential-congressional relations.[18] In the first, *partisanship*, split control can indeed lead to gridlock, as in the final two years of the Bush administration. But Jones concludes that gridlock was not inevitable—the perceived weakness of both sides led them to eschew compromise in favor of an all-out attack on the opposing party/institutional actor. In contrast, when both parties have acknowledged strengths, a pattern of *copartisanship* may develop, in which parties compromise their positions—even very different positions. Jones points to the 1990 budget deal as a prime example. Democrats swallowed budget cuts and accepted restraints they swore they would never accept, and Bush abandoned his "Read my lips, no new taxes" pledge.[19]

An even kinder, gentler form of executive-legislative relations is *bipartisanship*, by which Jones means that parties cooperate and com-

---

[16]Adler and Cameron, 24.
[17]Charles O. Jones, *The Presidency in a Separated System* (Washington DC: Brookings, 1994). Keith Krehbiel, "Institutional and Partisan Sources of Gridlock."
[18]Jones, 19–23.
[19]See also Weatherford's analysis of an earlier budget deal—national response to the 1958 recession. M. Stephen Weatherford, "Responsiveness and Deliberation in Divided Government: Presidential Leadership in Tax Policy Making," *British Journal of Political Science* 24(1994): 1–31.

promise in developing legislative proposals, and not just at the final passage stage of the process. Foreign relations, especially the Marshall Plan, under Truman and Congressional Republicans is the classic example. Finally, *crosspartisanship* occurs when a segment of one congressional party joins with the other party to form a majority. Thus, although it was formally divided, was the national government practically divided when the Southern "boll weevils" gave Reagan ideological control of the House in 1981 and enabled him to win passage of far-reaching budget and tax proposals? Although it was formally unified, was the government practically divided when defections by Southern Democrats blocked some parts of the agendas of Democratic presidents such as Roosevelt and Kennedy?

All-in-all, in his major extension of Mayhew's work, Jones finds little merit in the traditional argument that American government functions best when a strong president actively leads a Congress controlled by his party. Reading Jones' account, any disinterested observer will find examples of ineffective and effective government, successful and unsuccessful presidents, and good and bad legislation, under both unified and divided governments.

Krehbiel arrives at strikingly similar conclusions via an entirely different route. He sets up a sequential game theoretic model of the national policy-making process, then solves the game for the equilibria that exist under different configurations of the institutional actors. The elements of the configurations in Krehbiel's formal model are (1) the position of the president, (2) the position of the median voter in the legislature, (3) the positions of legislators empowered by extra-majoritarian features of the national policy-making process—the one-third-plus-one legislator that makes a veto override impossible, and the two-fifths-plus-one legislator that makes a filibuster succeed. Krehbiel finds that divided or unified control makes little difference—under a wide range of parameter values, both unified and divided configurations have gridlock equilibria. Even when Krehbiel assumes (contrary to fact) that the majority party is perfectly cohesive, gridlock still characterizes the equilibria of the unified government game. Krehbiel does identify one important factor that determines legislative movement: the position of the *status quo ante*. Where the status quo is far from the preferences of all the important actors—president, party or legislature median, and filibuster and veto pivots—the legislature passes and the president signs legislation. But this happens either with divided or unified control!

Interestingly, the aforementioned empirical study by Adler and Cameron broadly supports Krehbiel's bottom line. In their analysis, party-related and presidency-related variables prove insignificant. They also report a significant impact for a variable intended to capture the hypothesized greater distance between a new governmental "regime" and the status quo, but the connection to Krehbiel's analysis seems tenuous.[20]

Divided Government and Executive-Legislative Conflict

The studies reviewed thus far examine the impact of divided government on legislative productivity: does divided control result in a lower level of legislative output? Such a clear, direct effect is not the only logically possible one, of course. As noted in Chapter 6, divided control might have other, more subtle, more indirect effects on the political process, such as raising the level of executive-legislative conflict. For example, the historical record clearly indicates that presidents veto more legislation when government is divided than when it is unified. Consistent with that record, President Clinton vetoed no bills during his first two years in office, whereas President Bush vetoed 25 during the preceding two years.

Sean Kelley recently has shown that inter-branch conflict on roll call votes is greater during periods of divided government. Policy agreement between the president and congressional majorities is more than 20 percent lower when the institutions are controlled by different parties.[21] Significantly, the effect seems to be a step func-

---

[20]Adler and Cameron interpret Krehbiel as predicting that, whenever control changes, a change from the status quo is likely. But a glance at Krehbiel's Figure 5 illustrates his general conclusion that a change in control can produce significant legislative change in some cases (regime 2), but no change in others (regime 3).

[21]Policy agreement is calculated from a subset of important votes included in *Congressional Quarterly's* presidential success scores. See Sean Q. Kelley, "The Institutional Foundations of Inter-Branch Conflict in the Era of Divided Government," *Southeastern Political Review*, forthcoming.

tion reflecting the presence or absence of control, not a linear function of the number of seats controlled by the president's party. These findings support Sundquist's argument that, under divided control, congressional majorities are loath to do anything that would enhance the president's standing; on the contrary, they will bring matters the president opposes to a vote precisely to demonstrate their disagreement.

On the other hand, examination of another Congressional arena—committee hearings—reveals no difference between unified and divided control. Paul Peterson and Jay Greene find that hostile questioning of executive branch witnesses has declined in the post-war period even as divided control has become more common.[22] Congressional members of the president's party have become friendlier over time, whereas congressional members of the opposition are no more hostile now than in earlier decades. Peterson and Greene suggest that the common perception of increased inter-branch conflict is a misperception. One way of reconciling Kelley's findings based on roll call votes, and Peterson's and Greene's based on committee hearings is to suggest that partisan conflict will be more likely to emerge in more public arenas such as the floors of the House and Senate, than in more private arenas such as the committee rooms.

Divided Government and the Substance of Public Policy

The sheer generation of legislation is not the only important question for critics of divided government; what the legislation accomplishes is equally or even more important. One recent study has tackled the much more difficult task of *evaluating* the output of government.

Epstein and O'Halloran consider the willingness of a legislature to delegate discretionary authority to the executive.[23] They analyze

---

[22]Paul E. Peterson and Jay P. Greene, "Why Executive-Legislative Conflict in the United States Is Dwindling," *British Journal of Political Science* 24(1994): 33–55.
[23]David Epstein and Sharyn O'Halloran, "Divided Government and the Design of Administrative Procedures," forthcoming.

a sequential game of the sort constructed by Krehbiel. In this game, the legislature has the first move, deciding (via authorizing statutes) how much discretion the agency will be permitted to exercise. The executive moves next, choosing an agency head whose preferences mirror its own. The agency moves last, establishing a policy within the bounds of its range of discretion. One of the propositions generated by the model is that the legislature grants broader discretion when its preferences are more similar to the executive's, a condition presumably highly correlated with unified government.[24]

Epstein and O'Halloran test the proposition by examining the association between control of government and Congressional alterations in discretionary trade authority between 1890 and 1990. Controlling for other variables that previous research has found to be important in trade policy making (e.g., unemployment and the price index), a change from unified to divided government has a significant restrictive effect on bureaucratic discretion. Inasmuch as discretion has a negative effect on protectionism (both in the model and in a parallel empirical analysis), it appears that divided control inhibits the executive's ability to conduct a free trade policy.

Although it is only one study of a single policy area, the Epstein and O'Halloran work is highly significant. In Chapter 6 I noted that Mayhew's analysis makes no attempt to judge the *content* of legislation. Epstein and O'Halloran are the first to do so in a systematic way. Trade legislation has been passed under both unified and divided control, but a different kind of legislation has been passed when government has been divided, and it has had differential policy impacts.[25] More work of this kind will do much to settle the argument between those who believe patterns of control matter and those who regard patterns of control as matters of little importance.

---

[24]This proposition provides some more precise theoretical basis for the substantive argument advanced on pages 103–106 regarding the negative effect of divided government on the functioning of iron triangles.

[25]For the curious, across the whole period trade legislation was more likely to be passed under unified government than divided government, .56 enactments per Congress for the former, .35 enactments per Congress for the latter. But in the post-World War II period studied by Mayhew, trade enactments were slightly more frequent under divided government.

Divided Government and Budget Deficits

As pointed out in Chapter 6, many observers attributed the huge deficits of the 1980s to divided government. More systematic research over a longer period of time raised doubts. What is the current state of opinion? The national experience of recent years does little to settle the question. President Bush and the Democratic Congress negotiated a budget package/tax increase in 1990 that significantly lowered the growth of the deficit. Whatever the electoral cost to Bush of violating his "no new taxes" pledge, most analysts judged the agreement to have been one of the significant accomplishments of his administration. In 1993, the Democratic Congressional leadership rammed through President Clinton's budget package/tax increase without a single Republican vote in either chamber. Whatever the electoral cost to Clinton of appearing to be an "old-fashioned pro-tax Democrat," most analysts judged the package to have been one of the significant accomplishments of *his* administration. The Bush tax increase is an example of what Jones calls *crosspartisanship*, the Clinton tax increase, an example of what Jones calls *partisanship*. Both are widely viewed as good policy, one was produced by divided government, one by unified government. At the national level the relationship is as unclear as before.

At the state level there is new evidence, and the picture is somewhat clearer. Two ambitious empirical studies conclude that divided government—at least a particular form of it—has generally negative effects on budget deficits. Alt and Lowry examine state budgets between 1968 and 1987.[26] Based on a combination of formal models of party and institutional interaction, they test three hypotheses about patterns of control and deficits: (1) states with unified control will react to budget shocks by adjusting revenues; (2) states with split branch control (one party controls the legislature, one the executive) will react with a mixture of revenue and spending adjustments; (3) states with split legislative control will be slower to react than states with other patterns of control. The findings for split branch

---

[26]James E. Alt and Robert C. Lowry, "Divided Government, Fiscal Institutions, and Budget Deficits: Evidence from the States," *American Political Science Review* 88(1994): 811–828.

control are inconclusive, but the others are not. Although Alt and Lowry find no general tendency for any pattern of control to produce chronic deficits, unified governments respond more quickly and more effectively to shocks, especially where they are subject to balanced budget constraints. States with split legislatures are slower to react, whether constitutionally constrained or not.

A similar but independent study by Poterba examines state budgeting in the deficit-ridden years of 1988–1992.[27] Whereas Alt and Lowry examine year-to-year changes, Poterba examines within-year adjustments. His conclusions are very similar. Unified governments react more quickly, generally on the tax side, and balanced budget requirements enhance the speed of reactions.

These complex empirical studies yield an intuitively plausible picture. Unified state governments (typically Democratic in the era studied) respond to deficits by raising taxes. Split branch governments (typically Republican governor/Democratic legislature) respond with a mixture of tax increases and spending cuts—neither branch can go it alone, and the inevitability of compromise is obvious to both branches. Split legislatures, however, are more likely to become gridlocked, as each chamber is tempted to try to outlast the other in a "war of attrition." Such findings suggest that the 1990s' rise in split state legislatures is not a positive development. And on a more retrospective note, such findings add credence to McCubbins' account of the deficit politics of the Reagan era, even if the national data are not statistically conclusive.[28]

Summary: Divided Control and Government Performance

Chapter 6 concluded that the stronger claims for the negative effects of divided government had little empirical support. Four years of

[27]James Poterba, "State Responses to Fiscal Crisis: The Effects of Budgetary Institutions and Politics," *Journal of Political Economy* 102(1994): 799–821.
[28]Mathew McCubbins, "Party Governance and U.S. Budget Deficits: Divided Government and Fiscal Stalemate," in Alberto Alesina and Geoffrey Carliner, eds., *Politics and Economics in the 1980s* (Chicago: University of Chicago Press, 1991): 83–111.

additional experience and research does not markedly change that conclusion. At the national level, in particular, there is little evidence that divided government alone can account for the perceived failings of the federal government. Some recent work does suggest that divided government may affect the substance of policy in undesirable ways, but studies of many more policy areas need to be done before a general conclusion to that effect can be sustained, and the degree of undesirability measured.

At the state level, there is less research, but it is more suggestive. When the experiences of the states are pooled, there is sufficient data to generate statistically significant differences in the direction predicted by critics of divided government: divided control, at least of the legislature, appears to exacerbate budgetary difficulties. Still, many factors other than divided control play a role, and there is no evidence that split branch government (one party controls both legislative chambers but not the governor's office) performs any worse than unified government.

Accountability under Unified Control: The Lessons of 1993–94

Chapter 6 noted that, over and above the disputable claim that divided government detracts from the efficiency and productivity of government, there is a more compelling argument that divided control confuses the lines of responsibility in American politics. With different institutions controlled by different parties, how can voters hold parties collectively responsible for their performance? Moreover, knowing that it is difficult for voters to assess responsibility, elected officials have less reason to worry about their performance. Even if they have nothing to show by way of tangible accomplishments, they can resort to the "blame game"—posture about what you support and blame the other party for your inability to deliver.

Certainly, the 1994 congressional elections are consistent with the notion that unified control enhances electoral accountability. For two decades election observers marvelled at the ability of Congressional incumbents to insulate themselves from larger issues of national policy and performance, but many of these incumbents evidently found their insulation insufficient in 1994. Speaker of the House Tom Foley, Judiciary Chair Jack Brooks, Senate Majority Leader heir-apparent Jim Sasser—these and many others found themselves too closely tied to the policies and performance of the Clinton administration for a majority of their constituents. As usual they ran, but this time they couldn't hide. Unified Democratic control may well have been the difference.

Still, it is easy to exaggerate the extent to which the election was dominated by an angry electorate exacting its revenge on the Democrats. That image takes too literally the earthquake, tidal wave, and tsunami metaphors that dominated post-election commentary. As noted in Chapter 9, a variety of important considerations underlay the election results. Certainly I will not be surprised if subsequent research shows that national issues and presidential performance affected the Congressional voting in 1994 to a greater extent than in other recent elections. But that still leaves open the question of *why?* Why were the Republicans able to "nationalize" the 1994 elections? Was the answer simply "unified Democratic control?" If so, why were they were not able to nationalize the 1978 elections against a floundering Carter administration? Do the 1994 results indicate that collective accountability was there all along, just lying dormant and waiting for unified control to revive it—despite the Republican's inability to capitalize in 1978—or was 1994 an aberration? If unified control has revived collective responsibility, then we might see an older pattern of politics reassert itself, a pattern wherein one party or the other expects to gain unified control in the presidential elections, and divided government occurs as a consequence of losing one or both Houses of Congress at the mid-term. If this were to happen, proponents of unified government will have the chance to test their beliefs against contemporary reality. As citizens, we can only hope that in such an eventuality the optimism of the advocates of unified government is justified. But for analysts, it is much too early to conclude either that the era of candidate-centered elections has reverted to an older party-centered era, or that, if it has, conditions will necessarily improve.

Conclusion: Divided Government or Divided Citizenry?

All-in-all there is little in either the political experience or the scholarly literature of the mid-1990s that supports the stronger claims of the critics of divided government. To the extent that effects can be identified at all, the effects of divided government appear to be quite limited. Critics and commentators have been overly quick to lay the blame for the perceived failings of governments on split party control, while ignoring other, more important factors.

Prominent among those other factors are the preferences of the U.S. people. If citizens overwhelmingly condemn budget deficits, but just as overwhelmingly oppose cuts in entitlements and/or increases in taxes, there is not much that even a unified government can do to reduce the deficit. If citizens want government to insure a zero-risk society, but resent bureaucratic intrusion and red-tape, they are unlikely to be satisfied with the regulatory process. If citizens want guaranteed health care for all, unrestricted choice of doctors and facilities, and lower premiums than they currently pay, they are unlikely to be happy with any conceivable national health care plan. Does it make sense to blame political-institutional processes for failing to satisfy incompatible wants?

Of course, the fault may lie with our leaders. After all, if we had knowledgeable, public-spirited, charismatic leaders who could educate voters, inform their preferences, and dispel the illusions and contradictions, then the political process would work better. Perhaps that is the case, but I will not hold my breath waiting for such leaders, and I suspect that there have been few of them in the past. Such demigods typically are created after-the-fact in the panegyrics of palace historians.[29] The times make the leader as much as the leader makes the times.[30]

---

[29]Students are always surprised to learn that, according to the 1960 American National Election Study, *before the election* citizens held Richard Nixon in higher regard than John F. Kennedy. Kennedy's victory owed more to the fact that he was a Democrat— then the majority party—than to his charisma.

[30]Stephen Skowronek, *The Politics Presidents Make: Political Leadership from John Adams to George Bush* (Cambridge, MA: Harvard University Press, 1993).

The electoral politics of the early 1990s have firmed up my belief that the prevailing dissatisfaction of Americans with their governments largely reflects their lack of agreement on what, if anything, should be done. If most people dislike the status quo, but different groups strongly disagree over what direction policy should move in, no one is going to be very happy with how government performs. Consider the suggestive data in Table 11-1. Over the course of the past generation, Americans' views of the power of the federal government have polarized. When Lyndon Johnson and the 89th Congress were adopting "Great Society" initiatives, a plurality of the electorate expressed satisfaction with the level of activity of the federal government, and a significant minority favored additional activity. In contrast, when Bill Clinton and the 103rd Congress were trying to pass a National Health Care plan, only a tiny minority were satisfied with the federal government as is, while large and equal-sized pluralities wanted to go in opposite directions. In both cases government was unified, but it acted in the former case and gridlocked in the latter. Probably an important difference was

Table 11-1   The Disappearing Center

Which one of these statements comes closest to your own views about governmental power today?

1. The federal government has too much power.

2. The federal government is using about the right amount of power for meeting today's needs.

3. The federal government should use its powers more vigorously to promote the well-being of all segments of the people.

	1964	1992
Too much	26%	39
About Right	36	12
More vigorously	31	40

the size of the center relative to the opposed extremes in the 1960s versus the 1990s.

Those who yearn for energetic, effective government might do well to shift their focus away from the simple question of party control to the more complicated question of how to build majorities for the ends they support. If both divided control and lack of government action reflect the absence of popular consensus, attention should shift toward explaining the lack of consensus. Does it reflect the waning of consensus-building actors such as parties and the waxing of consensus-destroying actors such as single-issue groups? Does it reflect the divisive effects of a conflict-obsessed media and the polarizing effects of ideologically extreme political elites? Or are these developments too, just symptoms, not causes? Or as typically is the case, both? In the final analysis we are talking about the ability of a heterogeneous nation to govern itself, and no single factor operating in simple, straightforward fashion will determine how well or poorly we do. Future research may yet show that unified party control has some positive effects on government performance, but I doubt that it will turn out to be a "magic bullet" that will solve the vexing problems facing the nation.

Should we abandon the study of divided government then? Is it just another perspective that at first seemed to illuminate the political world, but in the end proved to obscure more than it enlightened? Despite the existing evidence, I hesitate to go that far. For one thing, the evidence on the limited effects of divided government is itself limited by the context in which it was produced. With the exception of some budgetary data from the 19th Century, virtually all the evidence comes from the post–World War II period, a period in which the New Deal party system gradually decayed into the era of divided government. Perhaps in this period of weakening party loyalties, declining parties, and the rise of new issues and problems, unified versus divided control made no difference. But is it simply an accident that the great political realignments identified by historically oriented scholars are all associated with unified government?[31]

---

[31]Walter Dean Burnham, *Critical Elections and the Mainsprings of American Politics* (New York: Norton, 1970). James Sundquist, *Dynamics of the Party System* (Washington, DC: Brookings, rev. ed., 1983).

Jackson's Democracy captured the federal government in 1828 and held it for 12 years, setting a new policy direction after the political disarray of the 1820s. The gridlock of the 1850s was broken by Lincoln and the Republicans who took full control of the federal government in 1860 and maintained unified control for 14 years, while redefining the Union and charting a new course of economic development. The "era of no decision" came to an end with Republican capture of the federal government in 1896. They held it for 14 years, lost control for 8, then held it another 10, completing the alliance of government with business. Finally, FDR and the Democrats gained full control in 1932, held it for 14 years, and led the country into the modern world.

In each of these cases, unified control provided the political power to implement the mandate that the fact of unified control was thought to represent.[32] There is little or no historical evidence that the development of a popular consensus preceded unified control. Quite on the contrary, Lincoln received only 40 percent of the popular vote (in a four-way election). FDR ran on a rather conservative platform, even promising to balance the budget. He struck out in a new direction only after his election. In these historical cases it appears that unified control provided an opportunity for the victorious political party to forge a new consensus, acting first, then taking its record to the electorate. The only consensus before the election was that the existing leadership should be changed.

From this perspective, divided government is important, but it is not an independent variable in a simple causal chain, as many contemporary analysts have conceived it. Rather, its place in a causal argument is more complex. It is a facilitating factor, one that helps the country lurch through one of the transformations that history periodically requires of us.[33] Would the South have seceded if the Democrats had maintained blocking power in the Senate in the 1850s?[34] Would FDR have had his famous 100 days if he had con-

---

[32]David Brady, *Critical Elections and Congressional Policy Making* (Stanford, CA: Stanford University Press, 1988).

[33]Lawrence Dodd, "Congress, the Presidency and the American Experience: A Transformational Perspective," in James Thurber ed., *Divided Democracy* (Washington DC: CQ Press, 1991): 275–302.

[34]Barry Weingast, *Political Economy of Slavery* (Manuscript in progress, 1991).

tinued to face a Republican House majority led by Speaker Nicholas Longworth? No one can answer such counter-factual questions conclusively, but surely one could defend negative answers to questions like these.

Thus, there are at least two distinct possibilities. The first holds that divided government is only a symptom not a cause; where popular consensus exists both unified and divided governments will act on it. The second holds that unified government provides an opportunity for similarly unified political leadership to forge a popular consensus—not a guarantee, but an opportunity.

Looking ahead, the 1996 elections might shed some light on these alternative possibilities. At the present time, most observers expect the Republicans to gain seats in the House as a result of the continuing erosion of southern support for the Democrats, and retirements of Democratic incumbents in the Senate make regaining control of that body an uphill fight for the Democrats. If the Republicans were to cap off their 1994 resurgence with continued Congressional gains and capture of the Presidency, one might expect an emboldened party with unified control to move policy rightward. If the electorate were to register its approval by reelecting Republicans and maintaining unified control, their behavior would support the notion of unified control as facilitator of political change.

On the other hand, if the electorate were to reelect Bill Clinton in 1996, or elect a Republican president but get little by way of policy change, or get significant policy change but strip the Republicans of unified control in 1998 or 2000, their behavior would support the notion of divided government as symptom of popular dissensus.

As political scientists we should continue to observe and record. Our task is to analyze the evidence, refine the theoretical arguments, and construct the accounts that will inform our understanding of U.S. politics at the dawn of the new millennium.

INDEX

Note: Page numbers followed by *n* indicate footnotes.